EUGENE O'NEILL

Modern Critical Views

These and other titles in preparation

Modern Critical Views

EUGENE O'NEILL

Edited and with an introduction by
Harold Bloom
Sterling Professor of the Humanities
Yale University

CHELSEA HOUSE PUBLISHERS
New York ◇ Philadelphia

© 1987 by Chelsea House Publishers,
a division of Main Line Book Co.

Introduction © 1987 by Harold Bloom

Printed and bound in the United States of America

10   9   8   7   6   5   4   3   2

∞ The paper used in this publication meets the minimum
requirements of the American National Standard for Permanence
of Paper for Printed Library Materials, Z39.48-1984.

Library of Congress Cataloging-in-Publication Data

Eugene O'Neill.

   (Modern critical views)
   Bibliography: p.
   Includes indes.
   1. O'Neill, Eugene, 1888–1953—Criticism and
interpretation.   I. Bloom, Harold.   II. Series.
PS3529.N5Z634   1987   812'.52   86-24429
ISBN 0-87754-633-9 (alk. paper)

Contents

Editor's Note

This book gathers together a representative selection of the best criticism available upon the plays of Eugene O'Neill. The critical essays here are reprinted in the chronological order of their original publication. I am grateful to Eden Quainton and Rhonda Garelick for aid in researching this volume.

My introduction, after meditating upon O'Neill's relation to American literature and American life, centers upon his two masterworks, *The Iceman Cometh* and *Long Day's Journey into Night*. The chronological sequence of criticism begins with Lionel Trilling, the representative American critic during O'Neill's lifetime. Trilling, affirming O'Neill's genius, nevertheless prophesied (in 1936) O'Neill's career-long flaw: "The peace of the absolute can be bought only at the cost of blindness to the actual."

Doris Falk, studying O'Neill's final plays, is severe as to their limitations, yet conveys the grim strength of the dramatist's late realization that the self and its ideal are equal, each to the other and both to zero. In Arnold Goldman's overview of O'Neill's development, the playwright's spiritual agony is also identified with the futility of human personality when it confronts the universe of death, realm of the Freudian reality principal.

The Iceman Cometh is analyzed by Robert C. Lee as an antithetical representation of the fervors of the evangelical and the anarchistic, after which Travis Bogard traces O'Neill's stance toward American history in *Mourning Becomes Electra* and *Ah, Wilderness!*, the latter being also Thomas F. Van Laan's focus as he uncovers the darkness of what he rightly judges to be the dramatist's only mature comedy.

Jean Chothia returns us to *Long Day's Journey into Night*, studying the play's success in exploiting the dialogue and gesture of its four fated characters, each with his or her "own kind of stammering eloquence."

Four crucial early plays are surveyed by C. W. E. Bigsby, who finds in all of them a dominant image of constriction.

In the essay that concludes this book, Michael Manheim analyzes *A Touch of the Poet* and *More Stately Mansions* as fragments of a cycle, tragic visions of kinship that reflect the incessant ebb and flow of O'Neill's autobiographical agonies.

Introduction

I

It is an inevitable oddity that the principal American dramatist to date should have no American precursors. Eugene O'Neill's art as a playwright owes most to Strindberg's, and something crucial, though rather less, to Ibsen's. Intellectually, O'Neill's ancestry also has little to do with American tradition, with Emerson or William James or any other of our cultural speculators. Schopenhauer, Nietzsche, Freud formed O'Neill's sense of what little was possible for any of us. Even where American literary tradition was strongest, in the novel and poetry, it did not much affect O'Neill. His novelists were Zola and Conrad; his poets were Dante Gabriel Rossetti and Swinburne. Overwhelmingly an Irish-American, with his Jansenist Catholicism transformed into anger at God, he had little active interest in the greatest American writer, Whitman, though his spiritual darkness has a curious, antithetical relation to Whitman's overt analysis of our national character.

Yet O'Neill, despite his many limitations, is the most American of our handful of dramatists who matter most: Williams, Miller, Wilder, Albee, perhaps Mamet and Shepard. A national quality that is literary, yet has no clear relation to our domestic literary traditions, is nearly always present in O'Neill's strongest works. We can recognize Hawthorne in Henry James, and Whitman (however repressed) in T. S. Eliot, while the relation of Hemingway and Faulkner to Mark Twain is just as evident as their debt to Conrad. Besides the question of his genre (since there was no vital American drama before O'Neill), there would seem to be some hidden factor that governed O'Neill's ambiguous relation to our literary past. It was certainly not the lack of critical discernment on O'Neill's part. His admiration for Hart Crane's poetry, at its most difficult, was solely responsible for the publication of Crane's first volume, *White Buildings*, for

1

which O'Neill initially offered to write the introduction, withdrawing in favor of Allen Tate when the impossibility of his writing a critical essay on Crane's complexities became clear to O'Neill. But to have recognized Hart Crane's genius, so early and so helpfully, testifies to O'Neill's profound insights into the American literary imagination at its strongest.

The dramatist whose masterpieces are *The Iceman Cometh* and *Long Day's Journey into Night,* and, in a class just short of those, *A Moon for the Misbegotten* and *A Touch of the Poet,* is not exactly to be regarded as a celebrator of the possibilities of American life. The central strain in our literature remains Emersonian, from Whitman to our contemporaries like Saul Bellow and John Ashbery, and even the tradition that reacted against Emerson, from Poe, Hawthorne, and Melville through Gnostics of the abyss like Nathanael West and Thomas Pynchon, remains always alert to transcendental and extraordinary American possibilities. Our most distinguished living writer, Robert Penn Warren, must be the most overtly anti-Emersonian partisan in our history, yet even Warren seeks an American Sublime in his still-ongoing poetry. O'Neill would appear to be the most non-Emersonian author of any eminence in our literature. Irish-American through and through, with an heroic resentment of the New England Yankee tradition, O'Neill from the start seemed to know that his spiritual quest was to undermine Emerson's American religion of self-reliance.

O'Neill's own Irish Jansenism is curiously akin to the New England Puritanism he opposed, but that only increased the rancor of his powerful polemic in *Desire under the Elms, Mourning Becomes Electra,* and *More Stately Mansions.* The Will to Live is set against New England Puritanism in what O'Neill himself once called "the battle of moral forces in the New England scene" to which he said he felt closest as an artist. But since this is Schopenhauer's rapacious Will to Live, and not Bernard Shaw's genial revision of that Will into the Life Force of a benign Creative Evolution, O'Neill is in the terrible position of opposing one death-drive with another. Only the inescapable Strindberg comes to mind as a visionary quite as negative as O'Neill, so that *The Iceman Cometh* might as well have been called *The Dance of Death,* and *Long Day's Journey into Night* could be retitled *The Ghost Sonata.* O'Neill's most powerful self-representations—as Edmund in *Long's Day's Journey* and Larry Slade in *Iceman*—are astonishingly negative identifications, particularly in an American context.

Edmund and Slade do not long for death in the mode of Whitman and his descendants, Wallace Stevens and T. S. Eliot, Hart Crane and Theodore Roethke, all of whom tend to incorporate the image of a desired death into the great, triple trope of night, the mother, and the sea. Edmund Tyrone and Larry Slade long to die because life without transcendence is impossible, and yet transcendence is totally unavailable. O'Neill's true polemic against his country and its spiritual tradition is not, as he insisted, that: "Its main idea is that everlasting game of trying to possess your own soul by the possession of something outside it." Though uttered in 1946, in remarks before the first performance of *The Iceman Cometh,* such a reflection is banal, and represents a weak misreading of *The Iceman Cometh.* The play's true argument is that your own soul cannot be possessed, whether by possessing something or someone outside it, or by joining yourself to a transcendental possibility, to whatever version of an Emersonian Oversoul that you might prefer. The United States, in O'Neill's dark view, was uniquely the country that had refused to learn the truths of the spirit, which is that good and the means of good, love and the means of love, are irreconcilable.

Such a formulation is Shelleyan, and reminds one of O'Neill's High Romantic inheritance, which reached him through Pre-Raphaelite poetry and literary speculation. O'Neill seems a strange instance of the Aestheticism of Rossetti and Pater, but his metaphysical nihilism, desperate faith in art, and phantasmagoric naturalism stem directly from them. When Jamie Tyrone quotes from Rossetti's "Willowwood" sonnets, he gives the epigraph not only to *Long Day's Journey* but to all of O'Neill: "Look into my face. My name is Might-Have-Been;/I am also called No More, Too Late, Farewell." In O'Neill's deepest polemic, the lines are quoted by, and for, all Americans of imagination whatsoever.

II

Like its great precursor play, Strindberg's *The Dance of Death,* O'Neill's *The Iceman Cometh* must be one of the most remorseless of what purport to be tragic dramas since the Greeks and the Jacobeans. Whatever tragedy meant to the incredibly harsh Strindberg, to O'Neill it had to possess a "transfiguring nobility," presumably that of the artist like O'Neill himself in his relation to his time and his country, of which he observed that "we are tragedy, the most appalling yet written or unwritten." O'Neill's strength was never conceptual, and so we are not likely to render his stances into a single coherent view of tragedy.

Whitman could say that: "these States are themselves the greatest poem," and we know what he meant, but I do not know how to read O'Neill's "we are tragedy." When I suffer through *The New York Times* every morning, am I reading tragedy? Does *The Iceman Cometh* manifest a "transfiguring nobility?" How could it? Are Larry Slade in *Iceman* or Edmund Tyrone in *Long Day's Journey into Night*, both clearly O'Neill's surrogates, either of them tragic in relation to their time and country? Or to ask all this in a single question: are the crippling sorrows of what Freud called "family romances" tragic or are they not primarily instances of strong pathos, reductive processes that cannot, by definition, manifest an authentic "transfiguring nobility?"

I think that we need to ignore O'Neill on tragedy if we are to learn to watch and read *The Iceman Cometh* for the dramatic values it certainly possesses. Its principal limitation, I suspect, stems from its tendentious assumption that "we are tragedy," that "these States" have become the "most appalling" of tragedies. Had O'Neill survived into our Age of Reagan, and observed our Yuppies on the march, doubtless he would have been even more appalled. But societies are not dramas, and O'Neill was not Jeremiah the prophet. His strength was neither in stance nor style, but in the dramatic representation of illusions and despairs, in the persuasive imitation of human personality, particularly in its self-destructive weaknesses.

Critics have rightly emphasized how important O'Neill's lapsed Irish Catholicism was to him and to his plays. But "importance" is a perplexing notion in this context. Certainly the absence of the Roman Catholic faith is the given condition of *The Iceman Cometh*. Yet we would do O'Neill's play wrong if we retitled it *Waiting for the Iceman*, and tried to assimilate it to the Gnostic cosmos of Samuel Beckett, just as we would destroy *Long Day's Journey into Night* if we retitled it *Endgame in New London*. All that O'Neill and Beckett have in common is Schopenhauer, with whom they share a Gnostic sense that our world is a great emptiness, the *kenoma,* as the Gnostics of the second century of the common era called it. But Beckett's post-Protestant cosmos could not be redeemed by the descent of the alien god. O'Neill's post-Catholic world longs for the suffering Christ and is angry at him for not returning. Such a longing is by no means in itself dramatic, unlike Beckett's ironically emptied-out cosmos.

A comparison of O'Neill to Beckett is hardly fair, since Beckett is infinitely the better artist, subtler mind, and finer stylist. Beckett writes apocalyptic farce, or tragicomedy raised to its greatest eminence. O'Neill doggedly tells his one story and one story only, and his story turns out to be himself. *The Iceman Cometh*, being O'Neill at his most characteristic, raises the vexed question of whether and just how dramatic value can survive a paucity of eloquence, too much commonplace religiosity, and a thorough lack of understanding of the perverse complexities of human nature. Plainly *Iceman* does survive, and so does *Long Day's Journey*. They stage remarkably, and hold me in the audience, though they give neither aesthetic pleasure nor spiritually memorable pain when I reread them in the study.

For sheer bad writing, O'Neill's only rival among significant American authors is Theodore Dreiser, whose *Sister Carrie* and *An American Tragedy* demonstrate a similar ability to evade the consequences of rhetorical failure. Dreiser has some dramatic effectiveness, but his peculiar strength appears to be mythic. O'Neill, unquestionably a dramatist of genius, fails also on the mythic level; his anger against God, or the absence of God, remains petulant and personal, and his attempt to universalize that anger by turning it against his country's failure to achieve spiritual reality is simply misguided. No country, by definition, achieves anything spiritual anyway. We live and die, in the spirit, in solitude, and the true strength of *Iceman* is its intense dramatic exemplification of that somber reality.

Whether the confessional impulse in O'Neill's later plays ensued from Catholic *praxis* is beyond my surmise, though John Henry Raleigh and other critics have urged this view. I suspect that here too the influence of the non-Catholic Strindberg was decisive. A harsh expressionism dominates *Iceman* and *Long Day's Journey*, where the terrible confessions are not made to priestly surrogates but to fellow sinners, and with no hopes of absolution. Confession becomes another station on the way to death, whether by suicide, or by alcohol, or by other modes of slow decay.

Iceman's strength is in three of its figures, Hickman (Hickey), Slade, and Parritt, of whom only Slade is due to survive, though in a minimal sense. Hickey, who preaches nihilism, is a desperate self-deceiver and so a deceiver of others, in his self-appointed role as evangelist of the abyss. Slade, evasive and solipsistic, works his way to a more authentic nihilism than Hickey's. Poor Parritt, young and self-haunted, cannot achieve the sense of nothingness that would save him from Puritanical self-condemnation.

Life, in *Iceman*, is what it is in Schopenhauer: illusion. Hickey, once a great sustainer of illusions, arrives in the company of "the Iceman of Death," hardly the "sane and sacred death" of Whitman, but insane and impious death, our death. One feels the refracted influence of Ibsen in Hickey's twisted deidealizings, but Hickey is an Ibsen protagonist in the last ditch. He does not destroy others in his quest to destroy illusions, but only himself. His judgments of Harry Hope's patrons are intended not to liberate them but to teach his old friends to accept and live with failure. Yet Hickey, though pragmatically wrong, means only to have done good. In an understanding strangely akin to Wordsworth's in the sublime *Tale of*

Margaret (*The Ruined Cottage*), Hickey sees that we are destroyed by vain hope more inexorably than by the anguish of total despair. And that is where I would locate the authentic mode of tragedy in *Iceman*. It is Hickey's tragedy, rather than Slade's (O'Neill's), because Hickey is slain between right and right, as in the Hegelian theory of tragedy. To deprive the derelicts of hope is right, and to sustain them in their illusory "pipe dreams" is right also.

Caught between right and right, Hickey passes into phantasmagoria, and in that compulsive condition he makes the ghastly confession that he murdered his unhappy, dreadfully saintly wife. His motive, he asserts perversely, was love, but here too he is caught between antitheses, and we are not able to interpret with certainty whether he was more moved by love or hatred:

> HICKEY. (*Simply*) So I killed her. (*There is a moment of dead silence. Even the detectives are caught in it and stand motionless.*)
>
> PARRITT. (*Suddenly gives up and relaxes limply in his chair—in a low voice in which there is a strange exhausted relief*) I may as well confess, Larry. There's no use lying any more. You know, anyway. I didn't give a damn about the money. It was because I hated her.
>
> HICKEY. (*Obliviously*) And then I saw I'd always known that was the only possible way to give her peace and free her from the misery of loving me. I saw it meant peace for me, too, knowing she was at peace. I felt as though a ton of guilt was lifted off my mind. I remember I stood by the bed and suddenly I had to laugh. I couldn't help it, and I knew Evelyn would forgive me. I remember I heard myself speaking to her, as if it was something I'd always wanted to say: "Well, you know what you can do with your pipe dream now, you damned bitch!" (*He stops with a horrified start, as if shocked out of a nightmare, as if he couldn't believe he heard what he had just said. He stammers*) No! I never—!
>
> PARRITT. (*To* LARRY—*sneeringly*) Yes, that's it! Her and the damned old Movement pipe dream! Eh, Larry?
>
> HICKEY. (*Bursts into frantic denial*) No! That's a lie! I never said—! Good God, I couldn't have said that! If I did, I'd gone insane! Why, I loved Evelyn better than anything in

life! (*He appeals brokenly to the crowd*) Boys, you're all
my old pals! You've known old Hickey for years! You
know I'd never—(*His eyes fix on* HOPE) You've known me
longer than anyone, Harry. You know I must have been
insane, don't you, Governor?

Rather than a demystifier, whether of self or others, Hickey is revealed as a tragic enigma, who cannot sell himself a coherent account of
the horror he has accomplished. Did he slay Evelyn because of a hope—
hers or his—or because of a mutual despair? He does not know, nor does
O'Neill, nor do we. Nor does anyone know why Parritt betrayed his
mother, the anarchist activist, and her comrades and his. Slade condemns
Parritt to a suicide's death, but without persuading us that he has uncov-
ered the motive for so hideous a betrayal. Caught in a moral dialectic of
guilt and suffering, Parritt appears to be entirely a figure of pathos,
without the weird idealism that makes Hickey an interesting instance of
High Romantic tragedy.

Parritt at least provokes analysis; the drama's failure is Larry Slade,
much against O'Neill's palpable intentions, which were to move his surro-
gate from contemplation to action. Slade ought to end poised on the
threshold of a religious meditation on the vanity of life in a world from
which God is absent. But his final speech, expressing a reaction to Parritt's
suicide, is the weakest in the play:

LARRY. (*In a whisper of horrified pity*) Poor devil! (*A long-
forgotten faith returns to him for a moment and he mumbles*) God rest his soul in peace. (*He opens his eyes—with a
bitter self-derision*) Ah, the damned pity—the wrong kind,
as Hickey said! Be God, there's no hope! I'll never be a
success in the grandstand—or anywhere else! Life is too
much for me! I'll be a weak fool looking with pity at the
two sides of everything till the day I die! (*With an intense
bitter sincerity*) May that day come soon! (*He pauses
startledly, surprised at himself—then with a sardonic grin*)
Be God, I'm the only real convert to death Hickey made
here. From the bottom of my coward's heart I mean that
now!

The momentary return of Catholicism is at variance with the despair
of the death-drive here, and Slade does not understand that he has not

been converted to any sense of death, at all. His only strength would be in emulating Hickey's tragic awareness between right and right, but of course without following Hickey into violence: "I'll be a weak fool looking with pity at the two sides of everything till the day I die!" That vision of the two sides, with compassion, is the only hope worthy of the dignity of any kind of tragic conception. O'Neill ended by exemplifying Yeats's great apothegm: he could embody the truth, but he could not know it.

III

By common consent, *Long Day's Journey into Night* is Eugene O'Neill's masterpiece. The Yale paperback in which I have just reread the play lists itself as the fifty-third printing in the thirty years since publication. Since O'Neill, rather than Williams or Miller, Wilder or Albee, is recognized as our leading dramatist, *Long Day's Journey* must be the best play in our more than two centuries as a nation. One rereads it therefore with awe and a certain apprehension, but with considerable puzzlement also. Strong work it certainly is, and twice one has been moved by watching it well directed and well performed. Yet how can this be the best stage play that an exuberantly dramatic people has produced? Is it equal to the best of our imaginative literature? Can we read it in the company of *The Scarlet Letter* and *Moby-Dick, Adventures of Huckleberry Finn* and *The Portrait of a Lady, As I Lay Dying* and *Gravity's Rainbow*? Does it have the aesthetic distinction of our greatest poets, of Whitman, Dickinson, Frost, Stevens, Eliot, Hart Crane, Elizabeth Bishop, and John Ashbery? Can it stand intellectually with the crucial essays of Emerson and of William James?

These questions, alas, are self-answering. O'Neill's limitations are obvious, and need not be surveyed intensively. Perhaps no major dramatist has ever been so lacking in rhetorical exuberance, in what Yeats once praised Blake for having: "beautiful, laughing speech." O'Neill's convictions were deeply held but were in no way remarkable, except for their incessant sullenness. It is embarrassing when O'Neill's exegetes attempt to expound his ideas, whether about his country, his own work, or the human condition. When one of them speaks of "two kinds of nonverbal, tangential poetry in *Long Day's Journey into Night*" as the characters' longing "for a mystical union of sorts" and the influence of the setting, I am compelled to reflect that insofar as O'Neill's art is nonverbal it must also be nonexistent.

My reflection however is inaccurate, and O'Neill's dramatic art is considerable, though it does make us revise our notions of just how strictly literary an art drama necessarily has to be. Sophocles, Shakespeare, and Molière are masters alike of language and of a mimetic force that works through gestures that supplement language, but O'Neill is mastered by language and relies instead upon a drive-towards-staging that he appears to have learned from Strindberg. Consider the close of *Long Day's Journey*. How much of the power here comes from what Tyrone and Mary say, and how much from the extraordinarily effective stage directions?

TYRONE. *Trying to shake off his hopeless stupor.* Oh, we're fools to pay any attention. It's the damned poison. But I've never known her to drown herself in it as deep as this. *Gruffly.* Pass me that bottle, Jamie. And stop reciting that damned morbid poetry. I won't have it in my house! *Jamie pushes the bottle toward him. He pours a drink without disarranging the wedding gown he holds carefully over his other arm and on his lap, and shoves the bottle back. Jamie pours his and passes the bottle to Edmund, who, in turn, pours one. Tyrone lifts his glass and his sons follow suit mechanically, but before they can drink Mary speaks and they slowly lower their drinks to the table, forgetting them.*

MARY. *Staring dreamily before her. Her face looks extraordinarily youthful and innocent. The shyly eager, trusting smile is on her lips as she talks aloud to herself.* I had a talk with Mother Elizabeth. She is so sweet and good. A saint on earth. I love her dearly. It may be sinful of me but I love her better than my own mother. Because she always understands, even before you say a word. Her kind blue eyes look right into your heart. You can't keep any secrets from her. You couldn't deceive her, even if you were mean enough to want to. *She gives a little rebellious toss of her head— with girlish pique.* All the same, I don't think she was so understanding this time. I told her I wanted to be a nun. I explained how sure I was of my vocation, that I had prayed to the Blessed Virgin to make me sure, and to find me worthy. I told Mother I had had a true vision when I was praying in the shrine of Our Lady of Lourdes, on the little island in the lake. I said I knew, as surely as I knew I was kneeling there, that the Blessed Virgin had smiled and blessed me with her consent. But Mother Elizabeth told me

I must be more sure than that, even, that I must prove it wasn't simply my imagination. She said, if I was so sure, then I wouldn't mind putting myself to a test by going home after I graduated, and living as other girls lived, going out to parties and dances and enjoying myself; and then if after a year or two I still felt sure, I could come back to see her and we would talk it over again. *She tosses her head—indignantly.* I never dreamed Holy Mother would give me such advice! I was really shocked. I said, of course, I would do anything she suggested, but I knew it was simply a waste of time. After I left her, I felt all mixed up, so I went to the shrine and prayed to the Blessed Virgin and found peace again because I knew she heard my prayer and would always love me and see no harm ever came to me so long as I never lost my faith in her. *She pauses and a look of growing uneasiness comes over her face. She passes a hand over her forehead as if brushing cobwebs from her brain—vaguely.* That was in the winter of senior year. Then in the spring something happened to me. Yes, I remember. I fell in love with James Tyrone and was so happy for a time. *She stares before her in a sad dream. Tyrone stirs in his chair. Edmund and Jamie remain motionless.*

Curtain

Critics have remarked on how fine it is that the three alcoholic Tyrone males slowly lower their drinks to the table, forgetting them, as the morphine-laden wife and mother begins to speak. One can go further; her banal if moving address to herself, and Tyrone's petulant outbursts, are considerably less eloquent than the stage directions. I had not remembered anything that was spoken, returning to the text after a decade, but I had held on to that grim family tableau of the three Tyrones slowly lowering their glasses. Again, I had remembered nothing actually said between Edmund and his mother at the end of act 1, but the gestures and glances between them always abide with me, and Mary's reactions when she is left alone compel in me the Nietzschean realization that the truly memorable is always associated with what is most painful.

She puts her arms around him and hugs him with a frightened, protective tenderness.

EDMUND. *Soothingly.* That's foolishness. You know it's only a bad cold.

MARY. Yes, of course, I know that!

EDMUND. But listen, Mama. I want you to promise me that even if it should turn out to be something worse, you'll know I'll soon be all right again, anyway, and you won't worry yourself sick, and you'll keep on taking care of yourself—

MARY. *Frightenedly.* I won't listen when you're so silly! There's absolutely no reason to talk as if you expected something dreadful! Of course, I promise you. I give you my sacred word of honor! *Then with a sad bitterness.* But I suppose you're remembering I've promised before on my word of honor.

EDMUND. No!

MARY. *Her bitterness receding into a resigned helplessness.* I'm not blaming you, dear. How can you help it? How can any one of us forget? *Strangely.* That's what makes it so hard—for all of us. We can't forget.

EDMUND. *Grabs her shoulder.* Mama! Stop it!

MARY. *Forcing a smile.* All right, dear. I didn't mean to be so gloomy. Don't mind me. Here. Let me feel your head. Why, it's nice and cool. You certainly haven't any fever now.

EDMUND. Forget! It's you—

MARY. But I'm quite all right, dear. *With a quick, strange, calculating, almost sly glance at him.* Except I naturally feel tired and nervous this morning, after such a bad night. I really ought to go upstairs and lie down until lunch time and take a nap. *He gives her an instinctive look of suspicion—then, ashamed of himself, looks quickly away. She hurries on nervously.* What are you going to do? Read here? It would be much better for you to go out in the fresh air and sunshine. But don't get overheated, remember. Be sure and wear a hat. *She stops, looking straight at him now. He avoids her eyes. There is a tense pause. Then she speaks jeeringly.* Or are you afraid to trust me alone?

EDMUND. *Tormentedly.* No! Can't you stop talking like that! I think you ought to take a nap. *He goes to the screen door—forcing a joking tone.* I'll go down and help Jamie bear up. I love to lie in the shade and watch him work. *He*

forces a laugh in which she makes herself join. Then he
goes out on the porch and disappears down the steps. Her
first reaction is one of relief. She appears to relax. She
sinks down in one of the wicker armchairs at rear of table
and leans her head back, closing her eyes. But suddenly she
grows terribly tense again. Her eyes open and she strains
forward, seized by a fit of nervous panic. She begins a
desperate battle with herself. Her long fingers, warped and
knotted by rheumatism, drum on the arms of the chair,
driven by an insistent life of their own, without her consent.

Curtain

That grim ballet of looks between mother and son, followed by the
terrible, compulsive drumming of her long fingers, has a lyric force that
only the verse quotations from Baudelaire, Swinburne, and others in
O'Neill's text are able to match. Certainly a singular dramatic genius is
always at work in O'Neill's stage directions, and can be felt also, most
fortunately, in the repressed intensities of inarticulateness in all of the
Tyrones.

It seems to me a marvel that this can suffice, and in itself probably it
could not. But there is also O'Neill's greatest gift, more strongly present in
Long Day's Journey than it is even in *The Iceman Cometh*. Lionel Trilling,
subtly and less equivocally than it seemed, once famously praised Theodore Dreiser for his mixed but imposing representation of "reality in
America," in his best novels, *Sister Carrie* and *An American Tragedy*. One
cannot deny the power of the mimetic art of *Long Day's Journey into
Night*. No dramatist to this day, among us, has matched O'Neill in depicting the nightmare realities that can afflict American family life, indeed
family life in the twentieth-century Western world. And yet that is the
authentic subject of our dramatists who matter most after O'Neill: Williams, Miller, Albee, with the genial Thornton Wilder as the grand exception. It is a terrifying distinction that O'Neill earns, and more decisively in
Long Day's Journey into Night than anywhere else. He is the elegist of the
Freudian "family romance," of the domestic tragedy of which we all die
daily, a little bit at a time. The helplessness of family love to sustain, let
alone heal, the wounds of marriage, of parenthood and sonship, have
never been so remorselessly and so pathetically portrayed, and with a force
of gesture too painful ever to be forgotten by any of us.

LIONEL TRILLING

Eugene O'Neill

Whatever is unclear about Eugene O'Neill, one thing is certainly clear—
his genius. We do not like the word nowadays, feeling that it is one of the
blurb words of criticism. We demand that literature be a guide to life, and
when we do that we put genius into a second place, for genius assures us
of nothing but itself. Yet when we stress the actionable conclusions of an
artist's work, we are too likely to forget the power of genius itself, quite
apart from its conclusions. The spectacle of the human mind in action is
vivifying; the explorer need discover nothing so long as he has adventured.
Energy, scope, courage—these may be admirable in themselves. And in the
end these are often what endure best. The ideas expressed by works of the
imagination may be built into the social fabric and taken for granted; or
they may be rejected; or they may be outgrown. But the force of their
utterance comes to us over millennia. We do not read Sophocles or
Aeschylus for the right answer; we read them for the force with which they
represent life and attack its moral complexity. In O'Neill, despite the many
failures of his art and thought, this force is inescapable.

But a writer's contemporary audience is inevitably more interested in
the truth of his content than in the force of its expression; and O'Neill
himself has always been ready to declare his own ideological preoccupa-
tion. His early admirers—and their lack of seriousness is a reproach to
American criticism—were inclined to insist that O'Neill's content was
unimportant as compared to his purely literary interest and that he injured

---

From *Essays in the Modern Drama*, ed. Morris Freedman. © 1936 by the New
Republic. D. C. Heath & Co., 1964.

his art when he tried to think. But the appearance of *Days without End* has made perfectly clear the existence of an organic and progressive unity of thought in all O'Neill's work and has brought it into the critical range of the two groups whose own thought is most sharply formulated, the Catholic and the Communist. Both discovered what O'Neill had frequently announced, the religious nature of all his effort.

Not only has O'Neill tried to encompass more of life than most American writers of his time but, almost alone among them, he has persistently tried to *solve* it. When we understand this we understand that his stage devices are not fortuitous technique; his masks and abstractions, his double personalities, his drum beats and engine rhythms are the integral and necessary expression of his temper of mind and the task it set itself. Realism is uncongenial to that mind and that task and it is not in realistic plays like *Anna Christie* and *The Straw* but rather in such plays as *The Hairy Ape, Lazarus Laughed* and *The Great God Brown,* where he is explaining the world in parable, symbol and myth, that O'Neill is most creative. Not the minutiae of life, not its feel and color and smell, not its nuance and humor, but its "great inscrutable forces" are his interest. He is always moving toward the finality which philosophy sometimes, and religion always, promises. Life and death, good and evil, spirit and flesh, male and female, the all and the one, Anthony and Dionysus—O'Neill's is a world of these antithetical absolutes such as religion rather than philosophy conceives, a world of pluses and minuses; and his literary effort is an algebraic attempt to solve the equations.

In one of O'Neill's earliest one-act plays, the now unprocurable *Fog,* a Poet, a Business Man and a Woman with a Dead Child, shipwrecked and adrift in an open boat, have made fast to an iceberg. When they hear the whistle of a steamer, the Business Man's impulse is to call for help, but the Poet prevents him lest the steamer be wrecked on the fog-hidden berg. But a searching party picks up the castaways and the rescuers explain that they had been guided to the spot by a child's cries; the Child, however, has been dead a whole day. This little play is a crude sketch of the moral world that O'Neill is to exploit. He is to give an ever increasing importance to the mystical implications of the Dead Child, but his earliest concern is with the struggle between the Poet and the Business Man.

It is, of course, a struggle as old as morality, especially interesting to Europe all through its industrial nineteenth century, and it was now engaging America in the second decade of its twentieth. A conscious artistic movement had raised its head to declare irreconcilable strife between the creative and the possessive ideal. O'Neill was an integral part—indeed,

he became the very symbol—of that Provincetown group which represented the growing rebellion of the American intellectual against a business
civilization. In 1914 his revolt was simple and socialistic; in a poem in *The
Call* he urged the workers of the world not to fight, asking them if they
wished to "bleed and groan—for Guggenheim" and "give your lives—for
Standard Oil." By 1917 his feeling against business had become symbol-
ized and personal. "My soul is a submarine," he said in a poem in *The
Masses*:

> My aspirations are torpedoes.
> I will hide unseen
> Beneath the surface of life
> Watching for ships,
> Dull, heavy-laden merchant ships,
> Rust-eaten, grimy galleons of commerce
> Wallowing with obese assurance,
> Too sluggish to fear or wonder,
> Mocked by the laughter of the waves
> And the spit of disdainful spray.
>
> I will destroy them
> Because the sea is beautiful.

The ships against which O'Neill directed his torpedoes were the
cultural keels laid in the yards of American business and their hulls were
first to be torn by artistic realism. Although we now see the often gross
sentimentality of the *S.S. Glencairn* plays and remember with O'Neill's
own misgiving the vaudeville success of *In the Zone*, we cannot forget
that, at the time, the showing of a forecastle on the American stage was
indeed something of a torpedo. Not, it is true, into the sides of Guggenheim
and Standard Oil, but of the little people who wallowed complacently in
their wake.

But O'Neill, not content with staggering middle-class complacency by
a representation of how the other half lives, undertook to scrutinize the
moral life of the middle class and dramatized the actual struggle between
Poet and Business Man. In his first long play, *Beyond the Horizon*, the
dreamer destroys his life by sacrificing his dream to domesticity; and the
practical creator, the farmer, destroys his by turning from wheat-raising to
wheat-gambling. It is a conflict O'Neill is to exploit again and again.
Sometimes, as in *Ile* or *Gold*, the lust for gain transcends itself and

becomes almost a creative ideal, but always its sordid origin makes it destructive. To O'Neill the acquisitive man, kindly and insensitive, practical and immature, became a danger to life and one that he never left off attacking.

But it developed, strangely, that the American middle class had no strong objection to being attacked and torpedoed; it seemed willing to be sunk for the insurance that was paid in a new strange coin. The middle class found that it consisted of two halves, bourgeoisie and booboisie. The booboisie might remain on the ship but the bourgeoisie could, if it would, take refuge on the submarine. Mencken and Nathan, who sponsored the O'Neill torpedoes, never attacked the middle class but only its boobyhood. Boobish and sophisticated: these were the two categories of art; spiritual freedom could be bought at the price of finding *Jurgen* profound. And so, while the booboisie prosecuted *Desire under the Elms*, the bourgeoisie swelled the subscription lists of the Provincetown Playhouse and helped the Washington Square Players to grow into the Theatre Guild. An increasingly respectable audience awarded O'Neill no less than three Pulitzer prizes, the medal of the American Academy of Arts and Sciences and a Yale Doctorate of Letters.

O'Neill did not win his worldly success by the slightest compromise of sincerity. Indeed, his charm consisted in his very integrity and hieratic earnestness. His position changed, not absolutely, but relatively to his audience, which was now the literate middle class caught up with the intellectual middle class. O'Neill was no longer a submarine; he had become a physician of souls. Beneath his iconoclasm his audience sensed reassurance.

The middle class is now in such literary disrepute that a writer's ability to please it is taken as the visible mark of an internal rottenness. But the middle class is people; prick them and they bleed, and whoever speaks sincerely to and for flesh and blood deserves respect. O'Neill's force derives in large part from the force of the moral and psychical upheaval of the middle class; it wanted certain of its taboos broken and O'Neill broke them. He was the Dion Anthony to its William Brown; Brown loved Dion: his love was a way of repenting for his own spiritual clumsiness.

Whoever writes sincerely about the middle class must consider the nature and the danger of the morality of "ideals," those phosphorescent remnants of a dead religion with which the middle class meets the world. This had been Ibsen's great theme, and now O'Neill undertook to investigate for America the destructive power of the ideal—not merely the sordid ideal of the Business Man but even the "idealistic" ideal of the Poet. The

Freudian psychology was being discussed and O'Neill dramatized its simpler aspects in *Diff'rent* to show the effects of the repression of life. Let the ideal of chastity repress the vital forces, he was saying, and from this fine girl you will get a filthy harridan. The modern life of false ideals crushes the affirmative and creative nature of man; Pan, forbidden the light and warmth of the sun, grows "sensitive and self-conscious and proud and revengeful"—becomes the sneering Mephistophelean mask of Dion.

The important word is *self-conscious*, for "ideals" are part of the "cheating gestures which constitute the vanity of personality." "Life is all right if you let it alone," says Cybel, the Earth Mother of *The Great God Brown*. But the poet of *Welded* cannot let it alone; he and his wife, the stage directions tell us, move in circles of light that represent "auras of egotism" and the high ideals of their marriage are but ways each ego uses to get possession of the other. O'Neill had his answer to this problem of the possessive, discrete personality. Egoism and idealism, he tells us, are twin evils growing from man's suspicion of his life and the remedy is the laughter of Lazarus—"a triumphant, blood-stirring call to that ultimate attainment in which all prepossession with self is lost in an ecstatic affirmation of Life." The ecstatic affirmation of Life, pure and simple, is salvation. In the face of death and pain, man must reply with the answer of Kublai Kaan in *Marco Millions*: "Be proud of life! Know in your heart that the living of life can be noble! Be exalted by life! Be inspired by death! Be humbly proud! Be proudly grateful!"

It may be that the individual life is not noble and that it is full of pain and defeat; it would seem that Eileen Carmody in *The Straw* and Anna Christie are betrayed by life. But no. The "straw" is the knowledge that life is a "hopeless hope"—but still a hope. And nothing matters if you can conceive the whole of life. "Fog, fog, fog, all bloody time," is the chord of resolution of *Anna Christie*. "You can't see where you vas going, no. Only dat ole davil, sea—she knows." The individual does not know, but life—the sea—knows.

To affirm that life exists and is somehow good—this, then, became O'Neill's quasi-religious poetic function, nor is it difficult to see why the middle class welcomed it. "Brown will still need me," says Dion, "to reassure him he's alive." What to do with life O'Neill cannot say, but there it is. For Ponce de Leon it is the Fountain of Eternity, "the Eternal Becoming which is Beauty." There it is, somehow glorious, somehow meaningless. In the face of despair one remembers that "Always spring comes again bearing life! Always forever again. Spring again! Life again!" To this cycle, even to the personal annihilation in it, the individual must say "Yes." Man inhabits a naturalistic universe and his glory lies in his recognition of its nature and assenting to it; man's soul, no less than the stars and the dust, is part of the Whole and the free man loves the Whole and is willing to be absorbed by it. In short, O'Neill solves the problem of evil by making explicit what men have always found to be the essence of tragedy—the courageous affirmation of life in the face of individual defeat.

But neither a naturalistic view of the universe nor a rapt assent to life constitutes a complete philosophic answer. Naturalism is the noble and realistic attitude that prepares the way for an answer; the tragic affirmation is the emotional crown of a philosophy. Spinoza—with whom O'Neill at this stage of his thought has an obvious affinity—placed between the two an ethic that arranged human values and made the world possible to live in. But O'Neill, faced with a tragic universe, unable to go beyond the febrilely passionate declaration, "Life is," finds the world impossible to live in. The naturalistic universe becomes too heavy a burden for him; its spirituality vanishes; it becomes a universe of cruelly blind matter. "Teach me to be resigned to be an atom," cries Darrell, the frustrated scientist of *Strange Interlude*, and for Nina life is but "a strange dark interlude in the electrical display of God the father"—who is a God deaf, dumb and blind. O'Neill, unable now merely to accept the tragic universe and unable to support it with man's whole strength—his intellect and emotion—prepares to support it with man's weakness: his blind faith.

For the non-Catholic reader O'Neill's explicitly religious solution is likely to be not only insupportable but incomprehensible. Neither St. Francis nor St. Thomas can tell us much about it; it is neither a mystical ecstasy nor the reasoned proof of assumptions. But Pascal can tell us a great deal, for O'Neill's faith, like Pascal's, is a poetic utilitarianism: he needs it and *will* have it. O'Neill rejects naturalism and materialism as Pascal had rejected Descartes and all science. He too is frightened by "the eternal silence of the infinite spaces." Like Pascal, to whom the details of life and the variety and flux of the human mind were repugnant, O'Neill feels that life is empty—having emptied it—and can fill it only by faith in a loving God. The existence of such a God, Pascal knew, cannot be proved save by the heart's need, but this seemed sufficient and he stood ready to stupefy his reason to maintain his faith. O'Neill will do no less. It is perhaps the inevitable way of modern Catholicism in a hostile world.

O'Neill's rejection of materialism involved the familiar pulpit confusion of philosophical materialism with "crass" materialism, that is, with the preference of physical to moral well-being. It is therefore natural that

Dynamo, the play in which he makes explicit his antimaterialism, should present characters who are mean and little—that, though it contains an Earth Mother, she is not the wise and tragic Cybel but the fat and silly Mrs. Fife, the bovine wife of the atheist dynamo-tender. She, like other characters in the play, allies herself with the Dynamo-God, embodiment both of the materialistic universe and of modern man's sense of his own power. But this new god can only frustrate the forces of life, however much it at first seems life's ally against the Protestant denials, and those who worship it become contemptible and murderous.

And the contempt for humanity which pervades *Dynamo* continues in *Mourning Becomes Electra*, creating, in a sense, the utter hopelessness of that tragedy. Aeschylus had ended his Atreus trilogy on a note of social reconciliation—after the bloody deeds and the awful pursuit of the Furies, society confers its forgiveness, the Furies are tamed to deities of hearth and field: "This day there is a new Order born"; but O'Neill's version has no touch of this resolution. There is no forgiveness in *Mourning Becomes Electra* because, while there is as yet no forgiving God in O'Neill's cosmos, there is no society either, only a vague chorus of contemptible townspeople. "There's no one left to punish me," says Lavinia. "I've got to punish myself."

It is the ultimate of individual arrogance, the final statement of a universe in which sociey has no part. For O'Neill, since as far back as *The Hairy Ape*, there has been only the individual and the universe. The social organism has meant nothing. His Mannons, unlike the Atreides, are not monarchs with a relation to the humanity about them, a humanity that can forgive because it can condemn. They act their crimes on the stage of the infinite. The mention of human law bringing them punishment is startlingly incongruous and it is inevitable that O'Neill, looking for a law, should turn to a divine law.

Forgiveness comes in *Ah, Wilderness!* the satyr-play that follows the tragedy, and it is significant that O'Neill should have interrupted the composition of *Days without End* to write it. With the religious answer of the more serious play firm in his mind, with its establishment of the divine law, O'Neill can, for the first time, render the sense and feel of common life, can actually be humorous. Now the family is no longer destructively possessive as he has always represented it, but creatively sympathetic. The revolt of the young son—his devotion to rebels and hedonists, to Shaw, Ibsen and Swinburne—is but the mark of adolescence and in the warm round of forgiving life he will become wisely acquiescent to a world that is not in the least terrible.

But the idyllic life of *Ah, Wilderness!* for all its warmth, is essentially ironical, almost cynical. For it is only when all magnitude has been removed from humanity by the religious answer and placed in the Church and its God that life can be seen as simple and good. The pluses and minuses of man must be made to cancel out as nearly as possible, the equation must be solved to equal nearly zero, before peace may be found. The hero of *Days without End* has lived for years in a torturing struggle with the rationalistic, questioning "half" of himself which has led him away from piety to atheism, thence to socialism, next to unchastity and finally to the oblique attempt to murder his beloved wife. It is not until he makes an act of submissive faith at the foot of the Cross and thus annihilates the doubting mind, the root of all evil, that he can find peace.

But the annihilation of the questioning mind also annihilates the multitudinous world. *Days without End*, perhaps O'Neill's weakest play, is cold and bleak: life is banished from it by the vision of the Life Eternal. Its religious content is expressed not so much by the hero's priestly uncle, wise, tolerant, humorous in the familiar literary convention of modern Catholicism, as by the hero's wife, a humorless, puritanical woman who lives on the pietistic-romantic love she bears her husband and on her sordid ideal of his absolute chastity. She is the very embodiment of all the warping, bullying idealism that O'Neill had once attacked. Now, however, he gives credence to this plaster saintliness, for it represents for him the spiritual life of absolutes. Now for the first time he is explicit in his rejection of all merely human bulwarks against the pain and confusion of life—finds in the attack upon capitalism almost an attack upon God, scorns socialism and is disgusted with the weakness of those who are disgusted with social individualism. The peace of the absolute can be bought only at the cost of blindness to the actual.

The philosophic position would seem to be a final one: O'Neill has crept into the dark womb of Mother Church and pulled the universe in with him. Perhaps the very violence of the gesture with which he has taken the position of passivity should remind us of his force and of what such force may yet do even in that static and simple dark. Yet it is scarcely a likely place for O'Neill to remember Dion Anthony's warning: "It isn't enough to be [life's] creature. You've got to create her or she requests you to destroy yourself."

DORIS FALK

Fatal Balance: O'Neill's Last Plays

In 1939, six years after *Days without End,* O'Neill completed *The Iceman Cometh,* in 1940–41, *Long Day's Journey into Night,* and in 1943, *A Moon for the Misbegotten* and *A Touch of the Poet.* During the same general period—from about 1934 to 1943—O'Neill had been hard at work on two long cycles of plays to be called *A Tale of Possessors Self-Dispossessed* and *By Way of Obit.* Of the first cycle he completed first drafts of three double-length plays, *The Greed of the Meek, And Give Me Death,* and *More Stately Mansions.* Dissatisfied with the early drafts of these plays and too ill to undertake drastic revision, O'Neill destroyed the first two. Although he had intended the destruction also of *More Stately Mansions,* a typescript of that play survives (the manuscript version was destroyed with the other two plays). Of the second cycle, *By Way of Obit,* O'Neill completed only one one-act play, entitled *Hughie,* still extant but unpublished.

At one time O'Neill had placed *A Touch of the Poet* fifth in the *Possessors* cycle, but when he abandoned the latter he considered his last four plays to be a related series, arranged in the following order: *The Iceman Cometh, A Moon for the Misbegotten, A Touch of the Poet,* and *Long Day's Journey into Night.* The exact composition dates of these and the cycle plays are far from clear; some had been begun years before—*A Touch of the Poet* in 1928. We do know, however, that between completion of *Days without End* and this final group of plays about ten years had

From *Eugene O'Neill and the Tragic Tension.* © 1958 by Rutgers, The State University. Rutgers University Press, 1958.

elapsed in which O'Neill's thinking underwent a change that reflected the frustrations of the intervening years.

O'Neill returned in these last plays to acceptance of struggle and flight as inseparable from and intrinsic to the life process. Now there is no way out but death. The struggle in these plays is essentially the same as it had always been in his work: the conscious intellect at war with the unconscious drives, the laceration of love and hate in every close human relationship, and the desperate search for self among the masks. Flight from the struggle is still in the pursuit of one of these illusory masks—but here we see a difference.

At last O'Neill had come face to face with the inevitable question: What happens when, long before the end of the play, the fugitive becomes clearly conscious that flight is futile and the self-image false? When he learns that *all* self-images are illusions, and that furthermore they are projected by a self which is worthless, if it exists at all? Then the self and its ideal are equal—and both equal to zero. Instead of a pull from the self to the self-conception, resulting in action (wasteful though that action may be), we have a perfect equilibrium, resulting in paralysis. Then, indeed,

> the odds is gone,
> And there is nothing left remarkable
> Beneath the visiting moon.

The theme of *The Iceman Cometh* is the death that results—the "iceman" who comes—when the self-images which keep the characters alive become known to them as mirage. The action takes place in "Hope's back room," the back room and a section of the bar of Harry Hope's saloon. Here fifteen derelicts keep themselves alive on alcohol and the "pipe dream" that they have been or some day will be respectable. They all know, at least unconsciously, the truth about themselves and each other, but they know, too, the vital necessity of illusion. So each accepts the other at his own evaluation and demands the same acceptance. As long as this state of things persists, as it does throughout the first act (nearly half the play), the characters are treated as comic. Their self-deceptions are ridiculous but not unlovable affectations. It is in the second act that, as O'Neill said, "the comedy breaks up and the tragedy comes on."

The commentator on the action and the actual protagonist of the play is Larry Slade, an aging ex-Anarchist who has long since withdrawn from the Movement and from life. In act 1 Larry is comparatively happy. He has an image of himself as the philosopher-bum who observes life from the grandstand and waits only for death. He is proud that he can see what the others cannot: that "the lie of a pipe dream is what gives life to the whole misbegotten mad lot of us, drunk or sober. . . . Mine are all dead and buried behind me. What's before me is the comforting fact that death is a fine long sleep and I'm damned tired, and it can't come too soon for me."

Yet, Larry's final disillusionment is still to come, in the person of young Parritt, the eighteen-year-old ex-Anarchist who has betrayed the Movement and his own mother, whom Larry once loved. (In fact, the context hints that Parritt is Larry's son). Disillusion comes for the others in the person of Hickey (Theodore Hickman), the traveling salesman whose success they all envy.

Hickey arrives at the bar on Harry Hope's birthday, an occasion for one of his periodical binges, but instead of the gay and dissolute Hickey they all expect, he is serious and sober. He announces the reason for the change: He has at last found peace by facing the truth about himself. Gradually he shames his listeners into believing that they, too, will find peace if they destroy their illusions and see themselves as they really are. He persuades all except Larry to go forth into the daylight and attempt the social rehabilitation they have always promised themselves. One by one, however, they crawl back to the bar the next day, broken and defeated by inevitable failure. They have faced the truth, but it has robbed them of the last, pitiful trace of hope.

Now not even liquor can make them happy; their old friendships turn to antagonisms. Hickey realizes that his plan has failed, and in trying to explain the failure to himself and to them he reveals that he attained his state of "peace" by killing his wife, Evelyn.

Hickey has convinced himself that he killed his wife because he loved her and wanted to spare her unhappiness over his uncontrollable drunkenness and dissipation—but as he speaks, his real motive comes through. He hated Evelyn because no matter what he did she always forgave him, never punished him, was always faithful. His running gag with the boys at Hope's had been that Evelyn was betraying him "in the hay with the iceman," but this was only his own wishful thinking. She never gave him even this relief from his own guilt. Hickey killed Evelyn because that was the only way he could free himself from her eternal forgiveness and achieve the ultimate in self-punishment. For him, to commit murder was to commit suicide. He has already called the police at the time of his confession.

When the police have arrived, however, and Hickey is concluding his story, his guilt becomes too much for him to face. Ironically, he creates his own pipe dream by persuading himself that he was insane at the moment of the murder. Hickey's illusion is a blessing to his friends, for it restores their own. Now they can go back to their bottles, convinced that they knew Hickey was insane all the time and faced reality only to humor him.

But Larry cannot go back. He must listen to Parritt's confessions—in dramatic antiphony to Hickey's—of his hatred of his mother (caused chiefly by jealousy of her many lovers) which led him to betray her to life imprisonment. Parritt has already resolved upon suicide, but he forces Larry to support his resolution. After listening to Parritt's outpourings, Larry finally cries, "Go, get the hell out of life, God damn you, before I choke it out of you!" Parritt is relieved and grateful: "Thanks, Larry. I just wanted to be sure. I can see now it's the only possible way I can ever get free from her. . . . It ought to comfort Mother a little, too. . . . She'll be able to say, 'Justice is done! So may all traitors die!' "

The mother-spirit has destroyed another of her sons.

When Larry hears Parritt fall from the fire escape, "A long forgotten faith returns to him for a moment." At least Parritt had the courage of his conviction. But the death of Parritt is the death of Larry's last illusion about himself. "He opens his eyes—with a bitter self-derision." He is no longer the philosopher, but only another down-and-out bum.

> Be God, there's no hope! I'll never be a success in the grandstand—or anywhere else! Life is too much for me! I'll be a weak fool looking with pity at the two sides of everything till the day I die! . . . Be God, I'm the only real convert to death Hickey made here. From the bottom of my coward's heart I mean that now!
>
> (Act 4)

The objectivist (as Larry thought he was at first), who looks at both sides of everything until they have equal value, must be a paralyzed spectator, unable to take action in any direction; but when the "two sides" are the masks of himself and both are worthless illusions, perfectly balanced against each other, he is not even a paralyzed spectator; he is dead. In *The Iceman Cometh*, as in the earlier plays, life and the self are lost together, when the tragic tension between the selves is lost.

The two sides of himself that Larry has seen are his expansive and submissive self-images. The expansive is that of the Anarchist, the active participator in "the Movement." The submissive is seen in his drive toward self-destruction. If Larry had been able to give either of these selves the value of a reality, he would have been drawn toward one or toward the other, would have been able to act either in the direction of his political obligations or in the direction of death by suicide, as Parritt did. Since he is pulled in both directions at once, he can only withdraw from the struggle altogether and become a non-participating observer of himself as well as of life. In Jung's terms, Larry exemplifies the "equal distribution of psychic energy." In Horney's, he is the neurotic who finds a pseudosolution to conflict in "resignation: the appeal of freedom." When Larry himself discovers the unreality of his solution, there is nothing left for him but the living death which Kierkegaard called "the disconsolateness of not being able to die." Even his conception of physical death as a warm and comforting womb (the return to the Earth Mother) or as a Babylon where " 'tis cool beneath thy willow tree" is to him only another illusion. Nevertheless, death is the single solution to his dilemma, since only annihilation of the self can annihilate the dilemma. His very inability to propel himself actively toward this annihilation—to accomplish it through suicide—is also death.

The philosophical implications of Larry's position are just as interesting as the psychological. Behind Aristotle's ethical definition of character as "that which reveals moral purpose, showing what kind of things a man chooses or avoids," is the problem which exists in some degree for every self-aware person, as it does in the extreme for the neurotic: the problem of creating oneself, of forming one's own character. The preliminaries and the process of choosing, even though they may be unconscious, are as important as the choice itself and the responsibility which is its result. Larry's power of choice is brought to a standstill because he cannot accomplish the preparation for it. His is the problem of projecting value in a world devoid of absolutes—the "existential" dilemma: man's chief struggle is not with Something but with Nothing, not with Evil but with the valuelessness that is neither good nor evil. Once he has overcome this Nothing, has created his values, man is then free to act according to them (or even, knowingly, contrary to them), but he is completely responsible both for the values and the actions predicated upon them. Such utter self-contingency can be paralyzing; it provides freedom, but it is that terrifying freedom from which, as Erich Fromm points out, most of us feel compelled to escape.

In defense of this philosophy as a "humanism" Sartre has pointed out that it is as positive as it is negative—as hopeful as it is despairing—in that each man has not only the responsibility, but the opportunity, to create his own destiny, and that each individual is ultimately responsible for the destiny of mankind as a whole. O'Neill has not only placed Larry in the existential dilemma, but has made him see and live both sides of the dilemma itself. In his youth Larry dedicated himself to Anarchism, an affirmation of nothingness and chaos and of man's freedom to create his destiny; but in his old age he sees anarchy's opposite face, that negation which we call despair.

The Iceman Cometh was written in 1939 during a period of deep depression and anxiety for O'Neill which he attributed to the impending war. The most revealing of his statements about his mental attitude at this time is in one of his letters to Clark, in 1941. O'Neill had temporarily stopped work on the cycle "pending a return of sanity and future to our groggy world. . . . So much has happened without and within, since I started to write it. The stories of the separate plays aren't affected much, but the vision of life that binds them into a whole has bogged down in shifting uncertainties."

Certainly O'Neill recorded those shifting uncertainties in *Iceman*. They had obliterated the philosophy of *Bound East for Cardiff,* which O'Neill had called "the germ of the spirit, life-attitude, etc., of all my more important future work." In this early play O'Neill had seen man as the courageous hero of his tragic life struggle; now, in 1941, man had proved himself a coward and an idiot, clinging for life to the very delusions which had unmanned him. He is an object of disgust, but withal pitiful.

The years in O'Neill's life closest in mood to the despair of 1939 and the following years were those of 1911 and 1912. O'Neill had come again to the hopelessness and death longing that in those months of destitution at Jimmy the Priest's had driven him to attempt suicide. One of O'Neill's roommates at Jimmy's, a press agent named Jimmy Beith, killed himself in a jump from a window. A month or so afterward O'Neill tried to end his life by means of an overdose of veronal, but was discovered in time and revived at Bellevue. That act was the young O'Neill's culminating answer to all the frustrations and confusions of his life—the failure to find himself, the guilts and tensions within the family, illness, an unhappy marriage. (In 1912 he was divorced from Kathleen Jenkins, mother of Eugene, Jr., whom he had married in 1909.) There is a bitter reference to the attempted suicide in *Long Day's Journey into Night,* where O'Neill links it to the rumor that his grandfather had taken his own life. Again O'Neill is interpreting the drive toward self-destruction as a manifestation of the family fate. Correct or not, the interpretation was sadly corroborated in the suicide of his own son, Eugene, Jr.

So it was that on the arid plateau of *The Iceman Cometh* the only meaningful reality to O'Neill was that of his own past and the family pattern woven into that past and into the dismal present. At first he circled around biographical realism at some distance with his projected cycle of plays to be called *A Tale of Possessors Self-Dispossessed*. He intended the cycle to record the rise of an Irish family in America and its struggle to establish itself in conflict with the hostile and exploitative Yankees. Although this conflict provides the background for *A Touch of the Poet* the play's real theme is the same as that of *The Iceman Cometh*—the conflict between prideful illusion and shameful reality in a character who keeps his self-respect only by perpetuating the illusion. He is Cornelius—"Con" —Melody, an Irish immigrant whose father began life as "a thievin' shebeen keeper who got rich by moneylendin' and squeezin' tenants and every manner of trick." Once wealthy, however, Con's father bought a castle on an estate in Ireland and educated his son to be a gentleman. Since Con was never completely accepted by his aristocratic schoolmates or their families, his life becomes a constant rebellion against his humble origin on one hand and the snobbery of the gentry on the other. He never is certain where he belongs. He rejects the peasant in himself and yet affirms him, but each time he becomes aware of the peasant image he is driven to deny it and to assert the image of the arrogant aristocrat. Con falls in love with a peasant girl and marries her after she becomes pregnant. Then, as Major Cornelius Melody of the British Army, he leaves her on his father's estate and goes to the Napoleonic wars. He acquires a reputation as a courageous if hotheaded young officer, but is finally forced to leave the army in disgrace after killing a fellow officer in a duel over the latter's wife.

Con emigrates with his wife, Nora, and his daughter, Sara, and sets up as a tavern-keeper in a village near Boston. As a kind of travesty of his Irish past the tavern is the center of a "country estate" which includes surrounding land and a lake. When the play opens, however, twenty years after his arrival in America, Con has failed at his trade. The family are almost desitute and the business near bankruptcy, but Con still plays the role of Major Cornelius Melody. His speech and bearing are still those of the gentleman; he rides a handsome mare and on the anniversary of the battle of Talavera dons his old uniform. The play turns on a series of tableaux in which Con stands before the mirror in his officer's scarlet coat, reciting Byron, with all the histrionics of a James O'Neill in the role of Monte Cristo.

In America Con has suffered the same alienation from self and society that he experienced in Europe. He knows he is beyond the pale of the established Boston families, but refuses to be identified with the Irish immigrants. Con has given up any real aspirations to belong to Boston society except, of course, in his dream-world. But his daughter, Sara, has not. She loves and intends to marry Simon Harford, son of a wealthy Yankee capitalist (the same who is referred to in *Moon for the Misbegotten* as "Harder," and in *Long Day's Journey* as "Harker"). Young Harford has come out to the country to meditate and write in a cabin on Melody's property. When the play opens, he is ill in a room upstairs in the tavern and is being nursed by Sara. Simon, who never appears on-stage but is described in detail by Sara, is dimly suggestive of the young O'Neill of the 1911 *Iceman* period, living sick and disconsolate over the barroom at Jimmy the Priest's. In fact, the time of *A Touch of the Poet,* ostensibly 1828, is actually, in O'Neill's mind 1911, for Melody's tavern is frequented chiefly by old derelicts, who sponge drinks by providing the Major with an audience to keep his "pipe dream" alive.

That dream is encouraged most by Con's wife, Nora, and threatened most by his daughter. *A Touch of the Poet* follows the usual O'Neill allegorical pattern. The Father is Pride, Lust, and Greed (this applies to both Melody and the elder Harford); the mother is submissive love, and the daughter—like her predecessors Nina and Lavinia—is the tormented combination of the two. The play suffers from over-exposition of this theme. Every action is explained by the characters—the word *pride* itself appears in one form or another in the text sixty-three times, usually followed by *humiliation* or *shame.* O'Neill is not satisfied with having Con act out his ridiculous and pathetic illusions, but must always make him analyze them.

Con's image of himself as the gallant officer is, of course, doomed. It awaits only a test which will destroy it and leave behind a defeated wreck worthy of the cast of *Iceman.* The test comes when the elder Harford, shocked at his son's involvement with Sara, offers to pay Con a settlement if his family will relinquish any claims on Simon and will go away. This insult, following as it does a snub by Mrs. Harford earlier in the play, so infuriates Con that he rushes to the millionaire's home to challenge him to a duel. He is promptly thrown out by Harford's servants; the whole affair degenerates into a street brawl, broken up by the police, and the final blow to Melody's pride comes when he realizes that he has disgraced himself before Harford's beautiful wife, and that his bail has been paid by Harford himself. When Melody returns to the tavern, he is no longer "the Major," but the son of the Irish shebeenkeeper. In a thick brogue he speaks of the Major as dead, caricatures his own Byronic pose, and in a final melodramatic gesture, shoots not himself, but his horse. The symbolic meaning of the action hardly needs explanation, but we have it, anyway: Sara asks her father why he killed the mare, and he answers,

Why did the Major, you mean! . . . Wasn't she the livin'
reminder, so to spake, av all his lyin' boasts and dreams? He
meant to kill her first wid one pistol, and then himself wid the
other. But faix, he saw the shot that killed her had finished
him, too. There wasn't much pride left in the auld lunatic,
anyway, and seeing her die made an end av him.

(Act 4, A Touch of the Poet)

The wife, Nora, is a forgiving and browbeaten Earth Mother, who
while pitiable is still a little sickening in her mooning over the handsome
husband who has spent his life abusing her. True, the Irish peasant in Con
loves her in his way, but the Major despises her. She, too, analyzes herself
for the audience. When Sara accuses her mother of enslaving herself to
Con, Nora answers: "There's no slavery in it when you love! *Suddenly her
exultant expression crumbles and she breaks down.* For the love of God,
don't take the pride of my love from me, Sara, for without it what am I at
all but an ugly, fat woman gettin' old and sick!" (act 1). This is the bitter
truth behind her constant submission to and forgiveness of her husband—
but need we be told?

Sara represents both her father's "divil of pride" and her mother's
instincts for selfless love. Toward her father she feels the ambivalence of
love and hate, pride and scorn. She worships the idea of the Major—even
unconsciously imitating her father's pose at times; but the very discrepancy
between what her father might have been and what he is intensifies her
resentment. Some of the most powerful scenes in the play are those in
which father and daughter are engaged in an *agon* of hatred and self-
revelation. Con sees in Sara the peasant in himself—her clumsy movements, her large hands and feet—and tortures himself and her with his
jeers; on the other hand, she is the daughter of Major Melody, a lady of
gentle birth, whose reputation has been threatened. Sara, for her part,
must reconcile her inherited pride with her—also inherited—love. She will
love Simon, but not with the slavishness of her mother's love for Con.
With mixed motives of ambition and love Sara "allows" Simon to seduce
her, but as she yields to him discovers the selflessness of her mother's
kind of love. She, too, becomes starry-eyed and believes that at last
the devil of pride in her has been overcome. "Now it's dead, thank
God—and I'll make a better wife for Simon." And yet, a few seconds
later, she is weeping for the death of her father's illusions; the proud
Major was a part of her, too. Nora tries in her own way to comfort
Sara, and she—the mother—has the closing words of the play, "Shame

on you to cry when you have love. What would the young lad think of you?"

The theme of the cycle, however, is not the power of love but the transmission through the family of pride, avarice, and ruthless ambition. Simon Harford's mother has described at length the exploitative greed of the Harford family which parallels the pride and social ambition of the Melodys. There is no reason to suppose that these traits would not dominate the children of Sara and Simon. In fact, the irony is that of the extant plays, the one in which this theme culminates is *Long Day's Journey into Night*—never intended as part of the cycle. Its characters are the true descendants of Sara and Simon, compounded of the same illusions and greeds, and in each of them "a touch of the poet."

After a long struggle, O'Neill gave up the cycle of plays about the presumably imaginary Irish family when he found his final material in his immediate family, the subject of the posthumously published and produced *Long Day's Journey into Night*. *A Touch of the Poet* was contrived and melodramatic, but *Long Day's Journey* is genuine drama; in O'Neill's words, a play "of old sorrow, written in tears and blood." The old sorrow was real; the play re-creates the tortured secrets of O'Neill's own family. But the importance of *Long Day's Journey* as biography is minor (most of the facts revealed it in had long been known or guessed) compared to its value as a synthesis of all we have been saying about the man and his work. It is an epilogue—a subdued, heart-rending coda sounding the themes of the entire canon. For this reason it deserves separate interpretation [elsewhere].

The sequel to *Long Day's Journey*, *A Moon for the Misbegotten*, continues the story of James Tyrone, Jr., who represents O'Neill's older brother, James, Jr. In *Long Day's Journey*, "Jamie" is an alcoholic, seeking constant escape from his own inadequacies and from guilt toward his younger brother and his mother. His final refuge is in lechery, but he can find satisfaction only in ugly, oversized women, the prostitutes rejected by other men, who feed his self-hatred and his need for a mother-substitute. The love affair in *A Moon for the Misbegotten* is derived from *Long Day's Journey*, which defines Jamie's love, hatred, and guilt toward his mother and the desperate longing for her which drives him to Josie in *Moon*.

If *A Moon for the Misbegotten* is a part of James, Jr.'s biography, then as biography, it is a thing of pity and terror. But as drama, it is the veriest scratching in rat's alley. The first half (actually act 1) is a crude country-bumpkin farce, taking place outside the run-down shack of a tenant farmer in Connecticut. In the second half, as in *Iceman*, "the comedy breaks up and the tragedy comes on." The change in tenor is simply a change in point of view. The setting of act 2 is "the same, but with the interior of sitting room revealed"—and the interior of the characters also. Before, they were comic grotesques, seen by a detached observer; now they are revealed from their own subjective point of view as pathetic creatures of "sadness and loneliness and humiliation."

Pathos cannot save *A Moon for the Misbegotten* from the weakness of its outward situation—the theatrical cliché of clichés, for which there is no other word but corn. O'Neill added a few twists, anecdotes, and complications for interest and transition to the psychological, but the skeletal story concerns the attempt of the farmer and the farmer's daughter to save the old homestead from the clutches of a supposedly villainous landlord. To this antiquity, like insult to injury, O'Neill has added another: the vaudeville team of the big strong woman who chases a puny man around the stage with (a) a broom and (b) the threat of a smothering embrace in a pair of enormous arms and an appalling bosom. The crowning indignity is the use, as a sort of refrain, of the maudlin sob-tune, "My mother's in the baggage coach ahead." Thus the play begins with a minstrel show (there actually exists a minstrel tune that goes, "A mother was chasing her boy with a broom, she was chasing her boy 'round the room.") and ends with meller-drammer. And with all his early theatrical experience and his belief that "life copies melodrama," O'Neill certainly knew what he was doing. He drops us a hint when he has Hogan, the farmer, describe his scheme for trapping the landlord (forcing him into a shotgun wedding with his daughter): "It's as old as the hills. . . . But . . . sometimes an old trick is best because it's so ancient no one would suspect you'd try it" (act 1, *A Moon for the Misbegotten*).

As to the serious, or "subjective," side of the play, the revelations of the psychological problems of the characters fit perfectly—too perfectly—into the pattern of O'Neill's thought at this time: that balance between the opposite masks of self, that paralyzing suspension of all value, which is fatal to action and movement and signifies the end of life. This pattern is actually all there is to the play; for, whereas *The Iceman Cometh* has a story and reveals living characters in conflict with themselves and each other, the story of *A Moon for the Misbegotten* serves only as a rack on which to hang—or stretch—the unconverted symbols of neurosis.

The three central characters of this play are New England Irish, with just enough Catholicism still clinging to them to provide expressive profanity. Phil Hogan is the farmer, his daughter is Josie, and Jim Tyrone, Jr., is the landlord whose family has long owned the Hogan farm. Hogan is a buffoon with a shrewd, coarse sense of humor but a soft heart, who serves in the plot largely as a kind of *deus ex machina* to bring the lovers together. On the pretext that Tyrone is planning to sell the farm to a neighboring villainous "Standard Oil man," Hogan persuades Josie to seduce Tyrone—then to blackmail him, by forcing him either to marry her or to pay Hogan the price of the farm to avoid scandal. However, Hogan reveals later that he knew Tyrone had no intention of selling the farm, and he (Hogan) only wanted to bring the two together so that they would recognize their hidden love for each other—a rather sad piece of hokum.

The story belongs, of course, to the misbegotten lovers, Josie, "so oversize for a woman that she is almost a freak," and Tyrone, the hopeless alcoholic, who finds, at least for one night, a mother and a lover in Josie. Unlike the men in *The Iceman Cometh,* Josie and Tyrone are protected by no lasting illusions about themselves. Josie's kindest "pipe dream" is her boast that she is a slut, who has slept with all the men in the neighborhood. But even she is aware of the truth of Jim's accusation that it is her "pride" which makes her affect this pose: that she is actually a virgin, longing to transcend her gross flesh in a spiritual love, but ashamed of this purity which seems too incongruous in a "great, ugly cow" of a woman.

When Tyrone attempts to confront Josie with this picture of her "submissive" self as a virgin, she refuses to admit the truth of the picture. To her denial Tyrone replies, "Pride is the sin by which the angels fell. Are you going to keep that up—with me?" (act 3, *A Moon for the Misbegotten*). O'Neill knew well the close relationship between self-hatred and neurotic pride. To overcome her hatred of that empirical "oversize" self which she can see, Josie has erected a more acceptable one which at least makes her an expansive, forceful character: feeling unlovable, she proves to herself that she can make men desire her, and in that process rejects the mixture of mother and virgin which Tyrone discovers that she really is.

Tyrone reveals Josie's position and his own when he says:

> You can take the truth, Josie—from me. Because you and I belong to the same club. We can kid the world but we can't fool ourselves, like most people, no matter what we do—nor escape ourselves no matter where we run away. Whether it's the bottom of a bottle, or a South Sea Island, we'd find our own ghosts there waiting to greet us—"sleepless with pale commemorative eyes," as Rossetti wrote. . . . You don't ask how I saw through your bluff, Josie. You pretend too much.
>
> (Act 3, *A Moon for the Misbegotten*)

But Josie is healthy enough to see and accept her conflicting selves for what they are: to be the virgin mother to Tyrone and resume her play-acting role of neighborhood slut when he has gone. She is another Cybel, with enough earthy animal love of life to go on living in spite of her difficulties, to meet the problems of everyday life through the haze of sadness and frustration that hangs over her. She has the "hopeless hope" that springs from Cybel's assumption of the inevitability of life opposites—between which her fate is still suspended, and in which she can still find some value and motion.

For Tyrone, on the other hand, there is no hope but in oblivion. He is probably the least dramatic of any of O'Neill's protagonists. His role in the play is one long self-analysis, one endless case history of self-hatred, alienation, neurotic conflict—all within the Oedipus configuration. Tyrone wears the same two masks as Jamie in *Long Day's Journey* (and as John Loving and Dion Anthony). His ravaged face has "a certain Mephistophe-lean quality which is accentuated by his habitually cynical expression. But when he smiles without sneering, he still has the ghost of a former youthful, irresponsible Irish charm—that of the beguiling ne'er-do-well, sentimental and romantic." In his sodden conversations with Josie he alternates between the coarse cruelty of a disillusioned lecher and the sweetness and simplicity of a little boy crying for his mother. Expansive at one moment, submissive at another, he does not know his real identity and withdraws from both self-images into the oblivion of drunkenness and the darkness of the womb—synonymous for him with tomb.

If the first glimpse of Tyrone reveals his disintegration within the masks of self, the second view of him is a study in self-hatred. At the end of act 2, when he has come to keep a date with Josie (and when *his* intentions are honorable, but hers are to seduce and then blackmail him), he is left for a few minutes alone on the stage.

> TYRONE: (*suddenly, with intense hatred*) You rotten bastard! (*He springs to his feet—fumbles in his pockets for cigarettes—strikes a match which lights up his face, on which there is now an expression of miserable guilt. His hand is trembling so violently he cannot light the cigarette.*)

Tyrone explains his guilt to Josie and to himself in terms of his lifelong hatred of his father and love and guilty longing for his mother. During his father's lifetime Tyrone was a drunkard and a ne'er-do-well, but after his father's death he stopped drinking for his mother's sake. "It made me happy to do it. For her. Because she was all I had, all I cared about. Because I loved her" (act 3, *A Moon for the Misbegotten*).

Then his mother became ill, and when Tyrone knew she was dying he turned to alcohol again: "I know damned well just before she died she recognized me. She saw I was drunk. Then she closed her eyes so she couldn't see, and was glad to die" (act 3, *A Moon for the Misbegotten*).

With his mother's death, all purpose and value departed from Tyrone's life, leaving him incapable of emotion, even of grief. He traveled across the country by train with his mother's body "in the baggage coach ahead," and spent his drunken nights with a prostitute he had picked up. Tyrone reduces his motives for this debauchery to vengeance upon his mother for leaving him. From that time on his life has been one long effort to obliterate his guilt and to punish himself not only for his behavior toward his mother, but for his feelings toward her, with their unconscious overtones of incest and hatred. Like so many of O'Neill's men, he hates the thing he loves—rebels against his dependency, then flagellates himself for having desecrated the mother-son (or man-woman) relationship.

When Tyrone comes to Josie, his one desire is for expiation. That same wronged maternal ghost who cried for vindication in *Desire under the Elms* and *Mourning Becomes Electra* must here again be laid to rest. In Josie's maternal and redemptive love for him Tyrone at last finds forgiveness and release. When he has confessed to Josie and discovers that he is still loved in spite of the hateful self he has revealed in the confession, Tyrone is absolved. The maternal spirit has been placated; now Tyrone can sleep, now he can die. All that remains is the fulfillment of the Earth Mother's final blessing: "May you have your wish and die in your sleep soon, Jim, darling. May you rest forever in forgiveness and peace." *A Moon for the Misbegotten* takes place in September, 1923. O'Neill's brother, James, died on November 8 of that year.

Tyrone is O'Neill's last little boy lost, crying for his mother. Whether or not he actually portrays James O'Neill, Jr., the relationship between him and Josie was O'Neill's final bitter and rather immature comment on the meaning of love. On the application of this view to O'Neill himself, his wife has had the last word. In an interview at the opening of *Long Day's Journey into Night*, Mrs. Carlotta Monterey O'Neill described "Gene's" courtship:

> And he never said to me, "I love you, I think you are wonderful." He kept saying, "I need you. I need you. I need you." And he did need me, I discovered. He was never in good

health. He talked about his early life—that he had had no real home, no mother in the real sense, or father, no one to treat him as a child should be treated—and his face became sadder and sadder.

ARNOLD GOLDMAN

The Vanity of Personality:
The Development of Eugene O'Neill

bitter: 1 a: having or being a peculiarly acrid, astringent, or disagree-
able taste suggestive of an infusion of hops that is one of the four basic
taste sensations 1 b: distasteful or distressing to the mind: *galling* 2:
marked by intensity or severity a: accompanied by severe pain or
suffering b: vehement, relentless also: exhibiting intense animosity c:
(1) harshly reproachful: sharp and resentful (2) marked by cynicism
and rancor d: intensely unpleasant esp. in coldness or rawness 3:
expressive of severe pain, grief, or regret.

—*Webster's Dictionary*

The underlying movement of an O'Neill drama—perceptible first in the
speech of characters, but extending equally to their relationships, to
episodes and to total structures—is a fluctuation and oscillation, a flow
and ebb forever turning back upon itself. It is the movement which L. C.
Knights, describing the language of *Macbeth,* has characterized as a "sickening see-saw rhythm."

This rhythm is found in individual characters either as a relationship
between portions of their speech or thought, or between speech and
thought. The easiest recognizable form is simple contradiction. Nina Leeds
broods to herself in *Strange Interlude* (1928):

Sam must give me a divorce ... I've sacrificed enough of my
life ... what has he given me? ... not even a home ... I had
to sell my father's home to get money so we could move near

From *American Theatre* (Stratford upon Avon Studies). © 1967 by Edward Arnold
Publishers Ltd. St. Martin's Press, 1967.

his job ... and then he lost his job! ... now he's depending
on Ned to get him another! ... my love! ... how shameless! ...

(*Then contritely*), Oh, I'm unjust ... poor Sam doesn't know
about Ned ... and it was I who wanted to sell the place ... I
was lonely there ... I wanted to be near Ned.

(Act 1)

Self-delusion perceived; admission, accompanied by remorse. Surface and
underlying reality approach efficient description of this and similar pendu-
lar motions in O'Neill only when the characteristic emotions are attached:
if the flow of self-justification originates in a feeling of being hurt and can
end in a hurting of others, the ebb has as the object of its animus only the
self.

All major O'Neill characters are divided against themselves, something which was already apparent to Mary Colum in 1935:

[O'Neill] has put with intensity on the stage one aspect of
American life that no other writer has managed to express at all
... that common character in American life, the disintegrated
person.
    [Strindberg's] disintegrated people were all madmen. But
O'Neill contrives to present his people as disintegrated and yet
holding on to sanity.

Not all of "his people"; the oscillation in Ella Downey, in *All God's
Chillun Got Wings* (1924), resonates out of control and becomes schizoidal.
She is torn to bits between a real love for her Negro husband Jim (if and
only if he remains subservient) and an equally real "*mean, vicious [and]
jealous hatred*" of him (act 2). She wants and does not want him to pass
his bar exams. As *both* poles of the rhythm acquire radical reality—one of
Nina's was a lie, even if the expression of a truly felt grievance—the
rhythm acquires dramatic complexity: Ella can love Jim if he fails in the
"white" world, partly because in so doing he remains for her the asexual
security to which she fled from that world, partly because it will preserve
him from her residual racial prejudice (Negroes should know their place)
at the same time as it confirms it (Negroes are not capable of rising), and
partly because he will then be the kind of failure she feels herself to be and
to deserve. Ironically, like Jay Gatsby trying to make himself over into the
social type he imagines Daisy Buchanan will desire, Jim is trying to

"become white" to satisfy Ella, to overcome his feelings of inferiority. The "resolution" the play allows Ella is a regression into childhood—"I'll be just your little girl, Jim" (act 2)—but her fragile, pitiful "happiness" leaves him baffled, blocked, in an intolerable position.

In Ella's regression, the ending of *All God's Chillun* is like those in many O'Neill plays. Similar are the regression to insanity in *Where the Cross Is Made* (1918/19), to savagery in *The Emperor Jones* (1920/21) and to "hopeless hope" in *The Straw* (1921). In each case, as in *Days without End* (1934), the regression appears as "the straw" at which the mind clutches to escape a situation of intolerable bafflement. The closest analogy to Ella Downey, however, is of course Mary Tyrone in *Long Day's Journey into Night* (1956, written 1939–41), whose mind leaps, under the influence of morphine, further and further into her past, reverting first (act 3) to her wedding day and then (act 4), "Back before she even knew me," as her husband James sadly admits, to her student days in the convent.

Mary Tyrone remains, however, sane, where Ella Downey does not, and the greater complexity of her speech-patterning is the measure, for us, of her sanity. Even at the outer limit of her "dope dream" the emotional variegation is still present—within the escape there is no escape—and her long monologue which ends the play, while it removes her entirely into her past, robs her at the last of fantasy-gratification. What she remembers is precisely the advice of Mother Elizabeth that precipitated her exposure to the world: that she leave the convent "for a year or two" to put "to the test" her wish to become a nun. Mary's barely submerged resentment preserves the troubled motion of her speech (and mind) to the very end.

Mary's language—and the structure of the play in so far as she helps comprise it—is a complex rhythm of admission and denial of her narcotic addiction, counterstressed with blame and exoneration of her husband James (for calling in the "quack" doctor who first gave her morphine to ease the pains of childbirth), her older son Jamie (for, as she imagines, having deliberately and fatally infected his brother Eugene with measles), and her younger son Edmund (whose birth, she claims, broke her health). Admission is excused by "the things life has done to us" and is even justified as a proof of the burdens of her life. But she meets with "*stubborn defiance*," and denial, the attacks on her which the others make, provoked as much by her own excuses and accusations as by their chagrin at once again having allowed themselves to believe her cured.

In two consecutively written plays, *Strange Interlude* and *Dynamo* (1929), O'Neill supplied his characters with "thoughts" as well as speech.

Here the added dimension can be seen working to the same purpose for more normative personalities than Ella and Mary Tyrone, troubling and upsetting the linear narrative flow. Kenneth Macgowan, writing in 1929, noted that "To the dramatic contrasts and conflicts of ordinary spoken dialogue O'Neill added the contrasts and conflicts of thoughts."

These "asides" spoken in *Strange Interlude* while all the characters "freeze" (the director, Philip Moeller's idea) have taken a beating from critics from the first performance on, and will do wherever the "contrasts and conflicts," the ruffling of verbal texture, is not recognized as their primary purpose. But the notion that the primary function of the asides in *Strange Interlude* is to reveal the true feelings which the characters otherwise hypocritically suppress is a stick to beat the play: where it is observed, the play can be called simplistic and, where it is not, O'Neill's failure to realize his intention. The fact is that the play is extremely outspoken in ordinary dialogue, and that, while Nina's father, the family friend Charlie and her husband Sam Evans are shockable, Nina—and Ned Darrell only to a lesser degree—is perfectly willing to shock. Nina and Ned's more acerbic "thoughts" are not different in kind from much of what they do say to others in the play.

The asides add, as Joseph Wood Krutch noted in his review, "depth" and "solidity," but they do it by obstructing what we would conventionally imagine to be the smooth flow of narrative—viz. what really gets said. (Some of the Theatre Guild, who first produced the play, wanted all the asides cut.) The play has a broken, dimensional movement; and the language, because of the ubiquity of the asides, can flow back and forth, poisoning itself and suggesting the dividedness of personality—not only split, but warring—"yet holding on to sanity." It is telling that the threat of insanity is held only over the healthiest (and dullest) mind in the drama, and the supposed hereditary taint never does visit him. Some of the characters, much of the time, are in highly emotional states, but the rhythms of those who are not are equally variegated by the technique. The play moves vertically as well as horizontally, and the verticals include half-heard and half-understood dialogue as well as the conscience, desire and further observation and reflection which constitute the asides. The structure follows a similar pattern, being the flux and reflux of Nina's spiritual fortunes: (down), up, further down, further up, etc.

Despite some clearly expressed and felt *truths*—as that (in the lines quoted at the beginning of this chapter) Nina Leeds really moved "to be near Ned"—it is significant that by about midpoint in the play, before the oscillations become so strong as to possess whole scenes radically, one almost loses any sense of what the "true selves" of the persons in *Strange Interlude* are. What do they really want and what are they really after? Does Nina love Ned, as she says? For a while it seems really doubtful, so capable are they of self-contradiction. This is a kind of dramatic modernity which the increasing hyperboles of fluctuation then drive out of the play; internal flux is externalized. For five acts Nina takes on a ruling passion for domination—for total control of "my three men" (act 1), for "one complete male desire . . . husband! . . . lover! . . . father!" (act 1). But in attempting to add "son" to this group, Nina overextends herself and in the last act all but the fantasy-father desert her.

The self-frustration of desire, the abandonment of one aim for another, larger one, and the discovery that what has been desired is, when attained, only a version of what was fled from, are similarly functions of the key O'Neill trope. There is a prime case of the third of these in *Dynamo*, where Reuben Light, in reaction against the stern religion of his minister-father, flees into the arms of the dynamo, only to discover that it is the same demanding God. It seems apparent that O'Neill's brother Jamie represented this type in life, and of the plays which levy most heavily on Jamie, *A Moon for the Misbegotten* (1947/52, written 1941–42)—written to give Jamie "his final due," said Carlotta O'Neill—presents the most extensive dramatic treatment of the subject.

Exhausted and near-derelict, Jamie Tyrone idealizes the giant farmer's daughter Josie Hogan as different from the class of women he knows best—whores. But his idealization leaves him unsatisfied, which—coupled with his knowledge of worldly attitudes—renders him cynical. Cynicism awakens desire for her, which can be countered by immediate revulsion, coupled with re-idealization or, if met by her acquiescence, assault on her as just another whore. The assault is then recognized as beyond reasonable measure, repented of, and the cycle begins again. It is really a parallel attitude to Nina Leed's desire for a "complete male desire": Jamie wants a mother *and* a whore.

In the mechanism behind Jamie, which produces the see-saw of emotion, the battle of attractions and repulsions, the operative terms are self-mockery, self-derision, self-defeat, self-laceration, self-torture—all terms used by O'Neill and the last of the masks of the ages of man worn in *Lazarus Laughed* (1927). Arthur and Barbara Gelb have recorded a revealing reminiscence of Carlotta O'Neill's which demonstrates that this complex was the particular involvement O'Neill himself experienced when writing *A Moon for the Misbegotten*:

> One night during the time O'Neill was working on the script
> [of *A Moon for the Misbegotten*], Carlotta was in her room
> listening to a Hitler speech on the radio. . . .
>
> "Gene came in and asked if he could lie down beside me
> and listen. . . . [He] was terribly distressed by it."
>
> When the speech was over, Carlotta tried to soothe her
> husband. Suddenly he sprang from the bed.
>
> "Goddam whore!" he shouted, and ran from the room.
>
> A few seconds later Carlotta heard him weeping in his own
> room. Controlling her mortification, she went to comfort him,
> and found him lying, face down on the floor.
>
> "He implored me to forgive him," Carlotta said. "He told
> me he hadn't known what he was saying, and explained that he
> had been reliving his days with Jamie—the days they had spent
> in whorehouses together."

The self-torment, which psychoanalysts—including G. V. Hamilton,
O'Neill's own—have related to unresolved Oedipal conflict and to "death-
wish," comprises a linguistic nexus for O'Neill's aesthetic and philosophical beliefs as well as his characterizations and his own personality. In an
interview of 1922 with Oliver M. Sayler, O'Neill said,

> The theatre to me *is* life—the substance and interpretation of
> life. . . . [And] life is struggle, often, if not usually, unsuccessful
> struggle; for most of us have something within us which pre-
> vents us from accomplishing what we dream and desire. And
> then, as we progress, we are always seeing further than we can
> reach.

And two years later he wrote in his playbill essay for the Provincetown
Players' production of Strindberg's *The Spook Sonata,*

> it is only by means of some form of 'super-naturalism' that we
> may express in the theatre what we comprehend intuitively of
> that self-defeating, self-obsession which is the discount we mod-
> erns have to pay for the loan of life.

Casting and rehearsal for *Welded,* O'Neill's first production in two
years—he had averaged three productions a year for the seven years
from 1916 to 1922—were then in progress. *Welded* has an upbeat ending,

underscored by its "stage directions": *"It is as if now by a sudden flash from within they recognized themselves, shorn of all the ideas, attitudes, cheating gestures which constitute the vanity of personality"* (act 2). But it is the "self-obsession" of modern, married life which is the play's subject. The two main characters are each surrounded by *"a circle of light"* which,

> *like auras of egoism, emphasize and intensify* ELEANOR *and* MICHAEL *throughout the play. There is no other lighting. The two other people and the rooms are distinguishable only by the light of* ELEANOR *and* MICHAEL.
>
> (Act 2)

The lighting is a direct theatrical use of "super-naturalism" to express "self-obsession." The problem, as it presents itself to the playwright-husband, is the apparent collapse of his "dream" of ideal, integrated marriage into what O'Neill was shortly to be calling, in his preliminary notes on the characterization of Electra in Greek drama, "undramatic married banality." Michael Cape cries in act 1 of *Welded*, "It seems at times as if some jealous demon of the common-place were mocking us" (act 2). After an act of tearing down, husband and wife exeunt to find consolation and satisfaction elsewhere, she with an old admirer (Act II)—an anticipation of Nina Leeds and Charlie Marsden—he with a prostitute (act 2)—an anticipation of Dion Anthony and Cybele in *The Great God Brown* (1926). From the prostitute Michael appears to receive a revelation:

> WOMAN. I was thinkin' of the whole game. It's funny, ain't it?
> CAPE. (*slowly*) You mean—life?
> WOMAN. Sure. You got to laugh, ain't you? You got to loin to like it.
> CAPE. (*this makes an intense impression on him. He nods his head several times*) Yes! That's it! That's exactly it! That goes deeper than wisdom. To learn to love life—to accept it and be exalted—that's the one faith left to us!
>
> (Act 2)

It looks like a "solution" has been found, but the counter-demands of his marriage flood back in act 3: the vanity of personality which desires domination, which fears loss of self, *versus* the need for union and for loss of mere self. Each conflicts with and cannot eradicate the other; alternatives are then entertained and rejected: they cannot part for good. A "modern," casual relationship is as dream-denying as any other sublunar solution—"If there's nothing left but—resignation!—what use is there? How can we endure having our dreams perish in this?" (act 2).

Despite the nominal happy ending (O'Neill often claimed that such endings were meant only as temporary respites), the total impression of the play is the non-ethical one of its title. Michael and Eleanor are "welded," not in permanent happiness, but in the cyclic rhythm of idealism, dissatisfaction, dissociation and return which is the play's completed structure. Haunting, the return of the curse of the old life, was against exorcism, the play's main positive thrust. (*Exorcism,* produced in 1920 but never published, is the title of O'Neill's play about his suicide attempt.) O'Neill's later, and last drama of modern married life, *Days without End,* ends with the actual casting-out of the cynical, life-denying *alter ego* "Loving" at the foot of the Cross.

That the self-defeat of an O'Neill hero is defeat of a "dream" is mirrored in a personal conflict between his sense of the mystery and wonder of life and his cynical revulsion from it, between romance and "reality." This conflict is directly posed in various plays and sophisticated, more disillusioning statements of it appear during the latter 'twenties—a stronger sense of the illusoriness of the romance. In *Marco Millions* (1927/28), after the Princess Kukachin has finally been disabused of her illusions about the materialistic Polo, the Emperor Kublai is moved to comment,

> My hideous suspicion is that God is only an infinite, insane energy which creates and destroys without other purpose than to pass eternity in avoiding thought. Then the stupid man becomes the Perfect Incarnation of Omnipotence and the Polos are the true children of God! (*He laughs bitterly*) Ha!
>
> (Act 2)

God abandons the side of romance and wonder and begins to appear on the other side, hitherto a god-less materialism. When in O'Neill's very next play, *The Great God Brown,* the self-torturing Dion Anthony, agreeing to prostitute his creative talent by working for the businessman Brown, follows him out of the room saying, "Lead on, Almighty Brown, thou Kindly Light!" (act 3), we witness an extrapolation of Kublai Kaan's "hideous suspicion." O'Neill's altering emphasis appears in Brown's stealing from Anthony the mask of his "creative life." It also appears, directly coupled with the "electricity" God, in the plot of *Dynamo*. In *Strange Interlude,* an incipient Manichaeanism enters with Nina Leeds's division of God into "God the Mother," the beneficent deity, and "God the Father," the maleficent. In a metaphor echoing Kublai's purposeless materialism, Nina calls life "the electrical display of God the Father" (act 1).

The discovery of "truth" gradually ceases to hold romantic promise in O'Neill. The antiphonal conflict of *Days without End*—"to get at the real truth" *versus* "nothing to hope for" when you find it (act 3)—contains the last suggestion that action will follow from intellectual discovery. In the next play, *The Iceman Cometh* (1946), the question is what to do with the horrible truth. The salesman Hickey believes that the inhabitants of Harry Hope's "hotel" should be made to see that their "pipe dreams" of re-entering ordinary life are illusions. But to Larry Slade, the derelict "Old Foolosopher" who believes they should be left alone in their dreams, Hickey is selling Death. In neither case are the dreamers going to "do" anything—it is only a question of whether the life of "tomorrows" is happier than one which knows there is no tomorrow.

The Iceman's action appears to bear Larry's out: the truth once discovered is quickly forgotten, a process facilitated by the revelation of Hickey's "personal" reason for his views (he has murdered his too-understanding wife.) But Larry is forced to abandon his own philosophy of near-apathetic non-interference by his undesired moral revulsion at Don Parritt's confession that he betrayed his mother to the police:

> LARRY. (*snaps and turns on him, his face convulsed with detestation. His quivering voice has a condemning command in it*) Go! Get the hell out of life, God damn you, before I choke it out of you! Go up——!
>
> (Act 3)

The imperative is thrust up from the depths: go upstairs and kill yourself—which Parritt does.

The double ending of *The Iceman Cometh* is ironically normative. Life mocks both extremes. There are limits to human nature in all directions: the truth-seller has an ineradicable ego conditioning his philanthropy (and besides, humanity cannot bear his kind of reality), and the quietist can arrive at a pass where options close and even he must admit involvement and play God.

II

The see-saw rhythm of dialogue is thus carried over into both the thematic content of plays and into their structures. In terms of character it creates radical ambivalences which become O'Neill's *forte* in the creation of characters (the more single-minded are nearer pasteboard figures). O'Neill came to found the very being of his people on ambivalences and polarities and he seems to have felt he could do without ordinarily conceived "true self" in characters—or even without the discovery of true self (by character or audience) as dramas unwind. If Jamie Tyrone's revelation of himself to his brother Edmund in the final act of *Long Day's Journey* appears to contradict this, it is in fact a revelation precisely of radical disintegration. What Jamie discovers is that he has *no* real self:

> Want to warn you—against me. Mama and Papa are right. I've been rotten bad influence. And worst of it is, I did it on purpose . . . to make a bum of you. Or part of me did. A big part. The part that's been dead so long. That hates life. . . . Wanted you to fail, Mama's baby, Papa's pet!
> . . . I love you more than I hate you. . . . I'd like to see you become the greatest success in the world. But you'd better be on your guard. Because I'll do my damndest to make you fail.
> . . . And when you come back [from the sanatorium], look out for me. I'll be waiting to welcome you with that "my old pal" stuff, and give you the glad hand, and at the first good chance I get stab you in the back.

It is a triumph of his "live" self that Jamie can, with the aid of drink, bring himself to discover this to Edmund, for it cannot do his announced motive any good. This triumph is yet another self-defeat and is, as Jamie himself knows, only momentary. Despite a classic "recognition scene," which we might expect to integrate Jamie, we continue to believe in the radical, self-destructive disunity of his soul.

From a very early point in his development, O'Neill appears not to have needed to work with heroes, or characters who would win through to positions of audience-shared satisfaction. In a letter of 1919, he wrote disparagingly to Barrett Clark of Smitty, the protagonist of *The Moon of the Caribbees* (1918), implying that his criticism is what constitutes the play's significance, while the more "heroic" treatment of the same character in *In the Zone* (1917/19) is a deficiency:

Smitty in the stuffy, greasepaint atmosphere of *In the Zone* is magnified into a hero who attracts our sentimental sympathy. In *The Moon*, poised against a background of that beauty, sad because it is eternal, which is one of the revealing moods of the sea's truth, his silhouetted gestures of self pity are reduced to their proper significance, his thin whine of weakness is lost in the silence which it was mean enough to disturb, we get the perspective to judge him—and the others—and we find his sentimental posing much more out of harmony with truth, much less in tune with beauty, than the honest vulgarity of his mates. To me, *The Moon* works with truth, and *Beyond the Horizon* also, while *In the Zone* substitutes theatrical sentimentalism.

What provided O'Neill with the "perspective to judge" in *Beyond the Horizon* (1920) was the decision to make Robert, the younger Mayo brother, stay on the farm and marry Ruth Atkins, though he desires the romance of the sea. O'Neill revealingly compared Robert Mayo with his antitype, the sentimental land-desiring sailor he had recently portrayed in *The Long Voyage Home* (1917):

At exactly the right moment, when I was floundering about in the maze of [*Beyond the Horizon*, Olson, who served as his model in *The Long Voyage Home*] . . . turned up in my memory . . . I thought, "What if he had stayed on the farm, with his instincts. What would have happened?" But I realized at once that he never would have stayed, not even if he had saddled himself with the wife and kids. It amused him to pretend he craved the farm. He was too harmonious a creation of the God of Things as They are. . . .

And from that point I started to think of a more intellectual civilized type—a weaker type from the standpoint of the above-mentioned God—a man who would have [an] inborn craving for the sea's unrest, only in him it would be conscious, too conscious, intellectually diluted into a vague, intangible, romantic wanderlust. His powers of resistance, both moral and physical, would also probably be correspondingly watered. He would throw away his instinctive dream and accept the thralldom of the farm for, why almost any nice little poetical craving—the romance of sex, say.

It is thus hard to doubt that the driving energy behind *Beyond the Horizon* was critical, just as the portrayal of the Olson-type in the play, Robert's elder brother Andrew, who does go to sea but for whom it means nothing, is basically critical. We watch a twin process of degeneration and deterioration, and Robert's recognition that only death can take him "beyond the horizon" is the play's only enlightenment. This scene, the last, was cut in the initial production, but restored by O'Neill to the published text, and he stressed, in occasional comments, that Robert's vision was to be taken seriously. Whatever that vision may imply (on a scale from delusion to mystical experience), it does not proceed developmentally from the bondage of the plot: it is release.

In "Eugene O'Neill: An Exercise in Unmasking," Eugene Waith has put the case for "development" in the plays:

> the characteristic movement . . . [is] toward discovery or revelation or both—a kind of unmasking.
>
> Toward the end of an O'Neill play there almost always comes a moment when the principal characters are for the first time fully revealed to the audience, and often it is only then that they fully understand themselves or their relationships to each other and to the world they live in. These recognition scenes are O'Neill's high points. . . . O'Neill seems to have thought of his characters' coming to terms with life as movement forward or back.

This view allows Waith to comment that *Desire under the Elms* (1924) depicts Eben Cabot and Abbie Putnam "mov[ing] through a sequence of false attitudes toward each other to true understanding and love." Yet it is possible that the web of life created by and for them leaves them no such release and that any positive state of mind in which the play may leave them cannot communicate itself to us so unambiguously.

Abbie murders her and Eben's child to "prove" her love for him, to prove she did not want a child to steal the farm Eben has so stolidly (and greedily) maintained was his by right. (Barrett Clark thought she would have murdered her husband, old Ephraim Cabot, instead.) Eben then turns her in to the police:

> EBEN. I woke him up. I told him. He says, "Wait 'til I git dressed." I was waiting. I got to thinkin' o' yew. I got to thinkin' how I'd loved ye. It hurt like somethin' was bustin'

in my chest an' head. I got t' cryin'. I knowed sudden I
loved ye yet, an' allus would love ye!

(Act 1)

Eben can now "love" Abbie precisely *because* he has just informed on her
(compare Don Parritt's betrayal of his mother in *The Iceman*) and because
he intends, as we discover momentarily, to share her punishment: "I got t'
pay fur my part o' the sin" (act 1). Regression and relaxation, masochism
and revenge may be absent from Eben and Abbie's minds, but not from
ours. The "love" here offers itself as another "poetical craving," not
exempt from the mire of "*ideas, attitudes [and] cheating gestures which
constitute the vanity of personality.*"

The ending of *Desire* shares its ambiguity between subjective elation
in the protagonists and wider, darker ramifications of their personalities
which the play has beforehand canvassed—and by which ramifications the
drama has obtained its tensile strength—with *Beyond the Horizon, The
Straw, Anna Christie* (1921/22), *Welded* and a number of later plays. If
Desire contains no technical facility (masks, unspoken thoughts—both to
make their appearance in the years immediately following) for showing
alternatives to what Abbie and Eben say they feel, it does surround them
with irony, Ephraim Cabot's—"Ye make a slick pair o' murderin' turtle-
doves" (act 1)—and the Sheriff's—the play's curtain-line, "It's a jim-dandy
farm, no denyin'. Wish I owned it!" (act 1). This ironical environment so
isolates the presumptive lovers that it almost deflects the tragedy into
"tragical satire." It is easy to imagine the mind which created Robert Mayo
being witheringly sardonic towards his turtle-doves; that the cynicism is
self-reflexive on "the world," which takes such views, does not impair its
force. O'Neill, as might be expected, took one and then another side in
public, nor are the dramas neutral—they do not project a synthesis of
sympathy and criticism, a view which makes both possible to an integrated
mind. If *Desire under the Elms* wins through, it is to a position of
ambiguity, a poise *between* false and true "attitudes" at the end. The
former cannot be discounted, nor the latter denied Eben and Abbie. This
ultimate ambivalence rids the play of injected "acceptance" and frees
O'Neill, on the other hand, from having to work with totally unredeemed
material.

The ambivalence is equally relevant to Lavinia Mannon in the trilogy
Mourning Becomes Electra (1931). The plays proceed by an ever-narrowing
series of options, whose necessary shrinkage is a measure of "Vinnie's" fate.
Each "event" in the plot is an attempt to bring about an *ending*, and each

time (until the last) unforeseen factors intervene to prevent any ending. Each time, as well, it comes to seem possible to choose between less and less. There were many possible reactions to the discovery of a mother's adultery—Vinnie's helps goad hers into the murder of her father. There is a more restricted range of reactions to a mother who has murdered your father—Vinnie drives hers to death, but has to account for the chagrin of her brother. With the brother Orin going mad and threatening her, Vinnie has a few alternatives left—to do as he wishes and live only with him, or to run off with Peter, or to find a way to marry Peter and stay where she is. She attempts the last; Orin dies; and so she is closer to freedom than she has ever been, but closer to "fate" as well. Peter deserts her, unable in his Puritanism to meet her at the passionate level she desires and needs. Love before everything, she is now crying, only to discover she has come full circle and is implicitly justifying the mother she had hounded to death. Her choice is now simple: she may walk out on her entire life in search of love (and in so doing admit she was wrong in persecuting her mother), or she may board herself up in the Mannon mansion, turning her back on the only thing in life she has come to desire, in fulfilment of her duty. Electra becomes Mourning.

When Lavinia does go inside, we may feel, with Eric Mottram, that her action sets the seal on the trilogy as "a modern masochistic play of self-punishment"; but we should also feel, at the cost of dividing ourselves, that her action was essentially right, necessary. "By the title," O'Neill insisted, "I sought to convey that mourning befits Electra; it becomes Electra to mourn; it is her fate; black is becoming to her and it is the color that becomes her destiny."

Mourning Becomes Electra, more than any play O'Neill wrote to 1935, does—if only by compounding them—avoid categories. That such evasion was uppermost in O'Neill's mind from the very start is demonstrable. To George Jean Nathan he wrote,

> It has been one hell of a job . . . to conjure a Greek fate out of the Mannons themselves (without calling in the aid of even a Puritan Old Testament God) that would convince a modern audience without religion or moral ethics; to prevent the surface melodrama of the plot from overwhelming the real drama . . . and finally to keep myself out of it. . . . [It is] a valid dramatic experience with intense tortured passions.

In a letter to the *New York Tribune* in 1921, O'Neill denied any necessity for Freudian or Jungian bases for the "psychology" of *Diff'rent* (1920/21), his first study of New England "repression" and violence. He was after, he claimed, "life that swallows all formulas." In its major thrust, the fate of Electra-Lavinia, *Mourning Becomes Electra* does bypass even Freudian categories.

There are moments, even scenes in O'Neill when formulization and even apparent polarities are felt to be abandoned for an undifferentiated totality of predicament. These moments are generally sprung out of extreme tension and blocked action, and occur in an interstice of time. The confrontation of Lavinia Mannon and her mother Christine is one such "moment": their relation may smack of a categorical Electra-complex, but the texture of their dialogue is sufficiently variegated to blot out simplicities.

Each seeks to dominate the other. It is a very uncomic version of the dialogue in *The Way of the World,* a "war game": advantages taken, pursued, attack overextended, retrenched, abandoned, defences maintained, counterattack. There is no merely theatrical exposition, as no item from the past (or the off-stage present) enters only to flesh out the "story." Each entry is part of the present battle.

Hughie (1958/59; written 1941) shows O'Neill's eventual total mastery of speech which is *making* a relationship rather than just stating its existence. "Erie" Smith, "a teller of tales," runs a wider, if less intense gamut than the Mannons, to win over *and* dominate the new night clerk of his sleazy West Side hotel. It is the conflict between winning over and domination which turns Erie's speech into a force-field: he is torn between despising the man's lack of Broadway "dope" and the need to enlist his companionship and sympathy. He berates, cajoles, flatters, in a complete cycle of attitudes whose spring, like the husband in *Welded,* is his need and his cynical reaction. In the end a fascinating cyclic symbiosis is attained and "life"—suspended for Erie since the death of the previous night clerk—can once more go on. The characters, like Lavinia and Christine Mannon and Erie Smith, who are involved in the agonies of suspended time need not understand "all" and are most certainly not above or outside their situations. It is interesting to reflect that *Bound East for Cardiff* (1916), the play which brought the unknown O'Neill to the notice of the then unfounded Provincetown Players, not only contains such a "moment," but is controlled by it, wholly polarized by the sheer fact of the dying sailor lying in his bunk. In a way, *Bound East* is Driscoll's, the onlooker's, play—as *Lazarus Laughed* is really Caligula's—and he and the dying Yank exist in a similar symbiosis as Erie and his two "Hughies."

The dialogue of Driscoll and of the other men, for whom he comes to stand proxy by virtue of his participation in the death agony, avoids, refuses to countenance the idea of death. (It assails them by threatening the "illusion" of sea-life by which they are sustained.) No one protests harder than Driscoll, and Driscoll does not break through to any clearer conception, much less to resignation and acceptance. It falls to the dying man himself to bring about a momentary *éclaircissement*, by admitting he is going to die. It is this admission—and not, as Kenneth Macgowan thought, "the fever of death"—which releases the flood of reminiscence and worry which brings the play to its ultimate articulacy. But the flood ironically takes Yank away from death to illusion—the dream of owning a farm—and again ironically, the illusion is nourishing, sustaining. The whole pattern of *The Iceman* and *Hughie* is already there, in 1916.

III

If the agony for an O'Neill protagonist was the struggle to break out of the "web," the nexus of fluctuation and ambivalence, to find a "faith" which was not regression and "pipe dream," it was in a manner O'Neill's problem, too. Success would mean the abandonment of the dramatic as it exists in the plays. Thus there is a sympathy for "failure" in O'Neill which grows apace with wilder dreaming and more incisive analysis of dream and ideal.

Lazarus is O'Neill's attempt at characterization of a man who had come through; and because he "had," nothing in the play tests him. Thus, the careful, act-by-act progression of deaths—his parents and relations (act 1), his followers (act 2), his wife (act 3), himself (act 4)—while obviously "structural," fails of dramatic tension. There is no pressure, let alone an increase of pressure, in any of these confrontations. Only the effect on Caligula, a recognizable self-torturing O'Neill type, incapable of sustained "belief," rescues *Lazarus Laughed* for drama.

For the caught character, in the long play, the effort is a search, and the "ending" takes on particular importance as a potential counter-weight to the "web." *Mourning Becomes Electra*, with its endings which turn out not to be endings, might have been titled *Days without End*, which O'Neill wrote next: it attempts parabolically the very question of "end" (termination, purpose).

O'Neill titled three of this play's four acts "Plot for a Novel." The hero, a novelist, is desperately searching for an 'ending' to the plot of *his* novel. That plot is a thinly disguised version of his own life, so he is also searching for a personal "end." That end, if it comes, will also be the end of O'Neill's play. *Days without End*, by means of this aesthetic analogy, is by way of being a transcript of O'Neill's process of creation, which is presented almost directly in the first scene, when John and "Loving," his visible *alter ego*, discuss possible "endings." John's predicament is similar to Michael Cape's in *Welded*, with the additional complication that a gratuitously committed adultery may alienate his wife if it is discovered.

The ending for which O'Neill settled, after many alterations, was religious conversion (to Catholicism). This is not illogical (as has been claimed), for it exists as an option—which Loving prevents—from early in the play. John has staked all on "married love" and it has not, he knows not how, prevented his adultery. (He cannot admit that "he" also hates his wife.) Some absolute outside marriage must stand as its guarantor—and this is the function of religion in the play, the force capable (as it turns out) of excluding the cynical self-hating portion of personality from life.

The ending is indeed melodramatic and naïve (in the context of the whole play), but possibly odder is the ambiguity caused by the "split-personality" device. (The business of masks in *The Great God Brown* may similarly end in confusion). Other characters besides "John" are allowed to hear "Loving," the denier, though only John can see him. That John, the "romantic" side of personality, would be unable to prevent Loving from "thinking" is a reasonable *donnée*, but that he (as visible deputy for the absent "whole" self) cannot prevent Loving from speaking out his cynicisms makes him seem altogether more schizoid than it appears he is to be taken. The others tut-tut John for "Loving's" interjections, but do not accept him for the tortured and radically disorganized person we do. If the point of making Loving audible was to display the other characters' insensibility to the protagonist's agony, it was done at the risk of making the protagonist a weaker man; but the weaker he is, the less final will we see his ultimate decision.

Days without End was not quite O'Neill's last attempt at the Way Up as a solution, but from 1935 the Way Down, the search for absolute bottom—not wholly absent from earlier plays—so energizes his work that it nearly transfigures itself into something like the "positive" value whose rejection begins it on its downward path.

The Gelbs have identified O'Neill's personal time of doing "his best to hit bottom" as "from early December of 1910 to May of 1911." This is the time in Argentina which the dying Yank in *Bound East* remembers with such fondness. But it is the other Yank, "the 'airy ape'" (1922), who explains to the real gorilla,

> I ain't on oith and I ain't in heaven, get me? I'm in de middle
> tryin' to separate 'em, takin' all de woist punches from bot' of

'em. Maybe dat's what dey call hell, huh? But you, yuh're at de
bottom. You belong.

(Act 3)

It is of course Yank's shaken belief in his own "belonging" which provides
the play's motive force, and the scenes which display his search up and
down "society" looking for a new place to belong (and muddling this with
revenge on his awakener) end only when "de bottom" is reached, and he is
crushed by a true ape.

"The bottom" reappears in 1928 as a "dive for the gutter," when Ned
Darrell interprets Nina Leeds's behaviour in the years just after the war-
time death of her *fiancé:*

> She's piled on too many destructive experiences. A few more
> and she'll dive for the gutter just to get the security that comes
> from knowing she's touched bottom and there's no farther to
> go!
>
> (Act 1)

Orin Mannon and Mary Tyrone state similar intentions, which flower as
Larry Slade's description of Harry Hope's:

> What is it? It's the No Chance Saloon. It's Bedrock Bar, The
> End of the Line Cafe, The Bottom of the Sea Rathskeller! Don't
> you notice the beautiful calm in the atmosphere? That's be-
> cause it's the last harbor. No one here has to worry about
> where they're going next, because there is no farther they can
> go. It's a great comfort to them. Although even here they keep
> up the appearances of life with a few harmless pipe dreams.
>
> (Act 3)

Ironically, Larry's picture is more wish than reality, in that the "harmless
pipe dreams" do cause "worry." Though Larry is for the others having
their dreams, he prides himself on having none and wishing for none: that
will be the ultimate "beautiful calm."

Larry mocks all hopes, ideals and faiths as "pipe" or "dope dreams,"
in the metaphor O'Neill had used as early as *The Straw* (act 3) and *The
Hairy Ape* (act 3), when his mother's narcotics addiction was still a
closely-kept secret. (Only the release of *Long Day's Journey* revealed it.)
The dope or (opium) pipe dream is a metaphoric intersection of hope,

ideal, fantasy and unconsciousness. These dreams are mocked and yet it is suggested that all life lives by them and that without them there is no life. There are, however, a cursed few, the self-tormentors, for whom the usual run of pipe-dreams is unsatisfactory, and for them only some final state of insentience, or "Nirvana," can minister. And there remains one final turn of the screw: the desire for insentience can turn out to be the biggest pipe-dream of all, and the one which gives, as a "dream," least satisfaction to the holder.

The state of total rest "begins" in a kind of mystical experience:

> EDMUND. I lay on the bowsprit, facing astern, with the water foaming into spume under me, the masts with every sail white in the moonlight, towering high above me. I became drunk with the beauty and singing rhythm of it, and for a moment I lost myself—actually lost my life. I was set free! I dissolved in the sea, became white sails and flying spray, became beauty and rhythm, became moonlight and the ship and the high dim-starred sky! I belonged, without past or future, within peace and unity and a wild joy, within something greater than my own life, or the life of Man, to Life itself; To God, if you want to put it that way. Then another time, on the American Line, when I was look-out on the crow's nest in the dawn watch . . . the moment of ecstatic freedom came. The peace, the end of the quest, the last harbor, the joy of belonging to a fulfillment beyond men's lousy, pitiful, greedy fears and hopes and dreams! . . . Like a saint's vision of beatitude. . . .
> *He grins wryly.*
> It was a great mistake, my being born a man, I would have been much more successful as a sea gull or a fish.

Edmund Tyrone's language gathers up O'Neill's previous touchings on the subject; Yank's ("belonging") and Larry Slade's ("the last harbor"). Eric Mottram has characterized this passage as "a sea ecstasy which [O'Neill] tried to make over into a religious experience . . . a central positive experience." Yet, as Mottram goes on to point out, Edmund's picture (in the context of his real present entrapment) is a "narcotic escape." Edmund's own phrase for it is that he is one of "the fog people" whose "native eloquence" is "stammering." The "fog person," like the pipe-dreamer, is an ambivalent conception—on the one hand the wanderer, lost between romance and reality, in the hell of this world; on the other, the person whose real element is an even peaceful, mistiness, beyond care and vexation.

The desire for total rest enters as early as *Strange Interlude*, when Nina Leeds, in the shambles of her failed dominations, succumbs to a regressiveness so powerful in its expression as to suggest something ultimate:

> Charlie will come in every day to visit . . . he'll comfort and amuse me . . . we can talk together of the old days . . . when I was a girl . . . when I was happy . . . before I fell in love with Gordon Shaw and all this tangled mess of love and hate and pain and birth began!
>
> (Act 1)

> You're so restful, Charlie. I feel as if I were a girl again and you were my father and the Charlie of those days made into one. I wonder is our old garden the same? We'll pick flowers together in the ageing afternoons of spring and summer, won't we? It will be a comfort to get home—to be old and to be home again at last—to be in love with peace together—to love each other's peace—to sleep with peace together——! (*She kisses him—then shuts her eyes with a deep sigh of requited weariness*)—to die in peace! I'm so contentedly weary with life!
>
> (Act 1)

Nina seems here not only to desire peace, but to have gained it, if in frustrated reaction and if at the cost of her vitality. The "strange interlude" is over.

From the peace of rest in *Strange Interlude* to a positive extinction of "ecstatic freedom" in *Long Day's Journey* and a negative desire for extinction in *The Iceman*—the spectrum adumbrates the climate of the Buddhist "Nirvana." That Nirvana represents an ultimate release from the antinomies of existence is undisputed, though whether it is a nihilistic and "negative" conception or a "positive" one is a matter of continuing debate.

When O'Neill used the word, he was concerned to associate it with "hope":

The Clerk's mind remains in the street to greet the noise of a far-off El train. Its approach is pleasantly like a memory of hope; then it roars and rocks and rattles past the nearby corner, and the noise pleasantly deafens memory; then it recedes and dies, and there is something melancholy about that. But there is hope. Only so many El trains pass in one night, and each one passing leaves one less to pass, so the night recedes, too, until at last it must die and join all the other long nights in Nirvana, the Big Night of Nights. And that's life.

(Hughie)

(O'Neill has finally merged his archaic Broadway slang and his romantic style into poetry.)

In *Beyond the Pleasure Principle*, Freud broached a dichotomy central to his later thought. The "pleasure principle," which he had earlier thought to be a uniform force of pain-avoidance, "the tendency to keep intracerebral excitation constant" (Breuer's phrasing; Freud), he now suggested could tolerate a rhythm of willed frustration and release. There was, however, a new principle, one in which the organism, in the grip of an autonomous force (ego-instinct) different from the sexual (object-instinct), willed a state of "Nirvana." Freud borrowed the phrase "Nirvana principle" from Barbara Low's *Psychoanalysis* (1920), and from it quickly grew his notion of the nature of destructive forces in personality and the controversial "death-instinct" in sentient matter. The "Nirvana principle," unlike the "pleasure principle," seeks only rest, vacuity, release from the cycle of existence into nonactivity.

In *Mourning Becomes Electra*, Vinnie and Orin had projected (and even visited) a "South Sea Island" as their escape from the Mannon "fate." O'Neill wrote his next two plays of "religious finality [and] tender family sentiment," *Days without End* and *Ah, Wilderness!* (1933) concurrently at Sea Island, Georgia. The last plays were all written at the "pseudo-Chinese" San Ramon, California home, "Tao House." The relations between Tao and Buddhism are complex and hardly unravelled, but it is often asserted that the spread of Buddhism into China was facilitated by Taoist concepts which resembled the "new" notions: "Thus for the Buddhist terms they coined Chinese equivalents. The Primal Nothingness (*pên-wu*) of Taoism prepared the way for the understanding of the Buddhist negativism of the Nonego, the Void and *nirvána*."

In interviews and letters to editors, O'Neill made "positive" claims for the bleakest of his early tragedies. According to him, the "poetical vision" of *Desire under the Elms* "illuminat[ed] even the most sordid and mean blind alleys of life." The emphasis falls on the "illumination." Perhaps O'Neill was bending over backwards to reassure the optimists: *Desire* was threatened with closure by the happy few for whom "pessimism" constitutes a clear and present danger to the American way of life. No such O'Neillian optimism is recorded apropos of the late plays. One may finally imagine, as Leslie Fiedler so unsparingly does of almost all major American writers, that O'Neill had "a secret message," an ultimate drift of hardly bearable toughness and dread—that the only supportable end of life is life's end, living or actual death, and that for the self-tortured there is only the Void. Worse still, the life instinct which was so baffled in its own search for faith, takes its revenge at the last by preventing the death-instinct's attainment of Nothingness: "Be God, there's no hope!" says Larry Slade, thinking of the now dead Don Parritt *"with a bitter self-derision,"* "I'll never be a success in the grandstand—or anywhere else!" (act 3). In the end, the drama and the bitterness are co-terminal. That the long disease of O'Neill's final, unproductive decade should have been a progressive degeneration of motor processes only, leaving his mind to function "normally," is, in relation to a lifetime of spiritual agony, almost too horrible even to contemplate.

ROBERT C. LEE

Evangelism and Anarchy
in The Iceman Cometh

With O'Neill one must always go back to *The Iceman Cometh,* for it is
both his culmination and his demise. *Long Day's Journey into Night* and
A Moon for the Misbegotten follow it, but more for personal purgation
than art. *Long Day's Journey* sums up O'Neill's life, while *Iceman* sums
up all life. "The *Iceman* is a denial of any other experience of faith in my
plays," O'Neill said in 1946. Earlier, in 1940, he had said, "There are
moments in it that suddenly strip the secret soul of a man stark naked." As
always, that naked soul was O'Neill himself.

For all its over-criticized length, *Iceman* is a play that has yielded but
slowly. Perhaps its sledgehammer nihilism has acted to block, indeed
confuse, understanding. There has been, for instance, fairly widespread
carping because the drunks in Harry Hope's saloon do not get drunk in any
normal way. Similarly, it has sometimes been bruited about that the
spiritual hardware salesman, Hickey, goes mad at the end of the play. Eric
Bentley, without question the leading detractor of *Iceman,* has mitigated
his attacks in recent years, but not by passing through the maze that
Iceman is. In his introduction to the play in *Major Writers of America,*
Bentley surmises that the play "ought to have been about Hickey's unresolved Oedipus complex," but it could not because "O'Neill's Oedipus
complex was unresolved. That at least is the interpretation which I wish to
submit for discussion." Bentley's former colleague at Columbia, Robert
Brustein, in *The Theatre of Revolt,* concludes his discussion by saying,

From *Modern Drama* 12, no. 2 (September 1969). © 1969 by the University of
Toronto, Graduate Centre for the Study of Drama.

"*The Iceman Cometh*, then, is about the impossibility of salvation in a world without God." If so, then what of love, that other fundamental impossibility in the O'Neillean world of icemen?

The play could be worked through O'Neill's life; that too has been tried. John Mason Brown even conjectured that Hickey symbolizes "Mr. O'Neill's subconscious protest against those who have chaperoned and tidied-up his own recent living." No doubt remains that O'Neill was at the end of his emotional tether in 1939. The onset of the war in Europe threw him into a depression from which he never wholly recovered: ideal romantic love failed him, his God remained dead (or died again), and his family past haunted him increasingly. O'Neill admitted as much, and more, himself. In a letter to Lawrence Langner of the Theatre Guild just after finishing *Iceman* he said: "To tell the truth, like anyone else with any imagination, I have been absolutely sunk by this damned world debacle. The Cycle [of plays] is on the shelf, and God knows if I can ever take it up again because I cannot foresee any future in this country or anywhere else to which it could spiritually belong."

O'Neill's biography is crucial, of course, but not in the way it is to *Long Day's Journey*. The latter could not have been written by anyone else, but *Iceman* could. Its affinity to both *The Lower Depths* and *The Wild Duck* has been clearly established. Indeed, it is in some ways easier to relate the literary stream to *Iceman* than it is to relate *Iceman* to O'Neill's own work, particularly his earlier plays. The imminent loss of faith and love, often seen as the same thing, is at the heart of all O'Neill plays, but that link does not tell us why Hickey hated his selfless wife Evelyn enough to kill her, nor why Don Parritt hated his anarchist-mother enough to betray her to the police, nor why Larry Slade hated life enough to become a convert to death. O'Neill went farther into that loss-of-self reality with *Iceman* than he had ever gone before. It leaves us at a loss.

What to do? Freud believed that it is possible for man to live in reality without illusions. With this thought in mind, let us begin with an overlooked statement of the meaning of *Iceman* by—not oddly—a psychiatrist, William V. Silverberg:

> Mankind, [O'Neill] says, is not yet ready for disillusionment; it is very far as yet from being mature enough to be set adrift from its moorings in religion and religion's handmaiden, a coercive morality. And—even more important—whoever attempts in this day and age to emancipate mankind from its illusions with haste, with impatience, with violence, is motivated not by love

of man nor by uncompromising devotion to reality, but by hatred and scorn of man, by bitterness, by a sadistic kind of mischief-making which has as its basis an inability to love anybody. . . . When men and women have truly learned to love one another, then they will be mature enough to dispense with religion and all coercive morality.

If one grants that disillusionment is a necessary stage, then O'Neill's characters are certainly not ready to go. Nor will they be for a long, long time. They are enchained by the life-destroying haters. And since the pipe dreamers fear death, which is also on the other side of the door of disillusionment, they shrink away into the pipe dreams at the bottom of the bottle. O'Neill wants man in reality, but, as Silverberg notes, he disavows hasty, impatient and violent emancipators. The two unifying symbols of this destructive encroachment, as we shall see, are the Anarchist Movement and evangelism.

Harry Hope's bar is the constricted world of total illusion, of life reduced to nothing. It is a final sanctuary from the busy world of salesmen and bomb-throwers outside. The "hope" in Harry Hope's name is ironic; it is the longing for undisturbed somnambulism. The derelicts who nurture pipe dreams from a rotgut whiskey bottle are not a composite Everyman, but only a shrinking shadow of Everyman on his fearful journey to death. Although each derelict has his own escape, together they function as a kind of Everychorus increasingly throughout the play. Taken together they represent mankind in "the last harbor," or, as Sophus Winther put it, "the antechamber to the morgue." The derelicts who are on ice are not entirely dead yet, for they maintain the appearance of life through harmless pipe dreams about either the past or the future. Until *Long Day's Journey,* a play in which "the past is the present" and "it's the future, too," O'Neill uses the past and the future as escape routes from the annihilating present. To the bums in "Bedrock Bar," the past and the future are interchangeable havens. Harry Hope, with his rinsed memory of his nagging wife Bessie, leads the "yesterday movement," while Jimmy Tomorrow leads the "tomorrow movement." "Worst is best here, and East is West, and tomorrow is yesterday," Larry Slade informs us at the outset of the play.

Into this "End of the Line Cafe" two dormant life forces come to renew their claims: the Movement and evangelism. Both have been here before, in the persons of Larry and Hickey, but only for escape. Now they come for purpose, and it is ironical that they are represented by betrayers; Hickey has betrayed God's law in killing his wife Evelyn and Don Parritt has betrayed the Movement in revenging himself against his mother, Rosa. Both Hickey and Don are too hasty, impatient, and violent. Hickey's effect on the derelicts and Don's effect on Larry will bear this out.

Sophus Winther is one of the few critics ever to deal with the all-important Movement, and he only briefly. In discussing the barroom bums he says, "Each in his own way was destroyed by his faith in the Cause, the Big Movement, the Ideal of what man should be." It is doubtful that this statement can be made to include all of the derelicts, but, surely, at the deepest level the Movement *does* represent an "Ideal of what man should be," as indeed the real late-nineteenth-century Anarchist Movement did. When Larry Slade, who has retired from the Movement because mankind doesn't want to be saved, learns of the arrest of Rosa and the West Coast anarchists he immediately senses a betrayal, and adds regretfully, "I'd swear there couldn't be a yellow stool pigeon among them" (act 1). Larry is himself an idealist in search of a disillusionment pipe dream, and his high regard for the honesty of the people in the Movement is an outgrowth of that not-dead yearning in him. But Larry is exceptional, as is the offstage Rosa, as was Hugo Kalmar, and—just possibly—Hickey and Don might be. None of the rest of the pipe dreamers possesses enough of a certain something, call it quest, ever to have had faith in a Cause, or to have left it in discouragement. Their spiritual blight came too early in life. To Everychorus, the Movement is irrelevant; they know instinctively that the way to the ideal is through the door of disillusionment, and they fear to go. "I'll make your Movement move!" (act 1) Harry Hope tells Larry in the perfectly disdainful voice of a non-reformer. And Joe Mott, the one-time "white" Negro, senses the underlying violence in the Movement when he says, "If [an anarchist] do ever get a nickel, he blows it on bombs" (act 1).

Hugo Kalmar, the has-been anarchist periodical editor and jail martyr, is a pitifully fascinating example of the Movement's inability to draw the ideal nearer to the real. Hugo loves the proletariat, but he retains the urge to be a God to them, as this typical sample of his drunken musings indicates:

> Hello, leedle peoples! Neffer mind! Soon you vill eat hot dogs beneath the villow trees and trink vine—(Abruptly in a haughty fastidious tone) The champagne vas not properly iced. (With guttural anger) Gottamned liar, Hickey! Does that prove I vant to be aristocrat? I love only the proletariat! I vill lead them! I vill be like a Gott to them! They vill be my slaves! (He stops in bewildered self-amazement).
>
> (Act 3)

Hugo suggests the class struggle between the aristocracy and the proletariat, but he is also the tattered remains of the Nietzschean Superman. He lacks Zarathustra's (and Hickey's) "right kind of pity," but he would like to have power anyway. Larry says of Hugo: "No one takes him seriously. That's his epitaph. Not even the comrades any more. If I've been through with the Movement long since, it's been through with him, and, thanks to whiskey, he's the only one doesn't know it" (act 2).

In one way Hugo's plight is the worst of the iced-men, for the magnitude of his crime of aristocratic longings has prevented him from joining either the "tomorrow" or the "yesterday" movement. His past and his future are only rotgut. It is for this reason that he, the nearest to death, is most fearfully aware of death's presence. There are two supreme moments when death is present on the stage in *Iceman*, and Hugo reacts to both of them. When Harry Hope returns from his abortive attempt to take a walk out into the world and finds that, after the horror of reality, his booze no longer has a kick in it, Hugo immediately recognizes that Hope is dead and refuses to sit at his table. At the other moment of death, after Don has leapt from the fire escape, it is Hugo who notices Larry's demise. Once again Hugo refuses to sit at a table of death. "Crazy fool!" he tells Larry in terrified anger. "You vas crazy like Hickey! You give me bad dreams, too" (act 4). To Hugo, Larry's ordering Don out of life is as frightening as Hickey's salvation pitch.

To the Judas of the piece, Don Parritt, the Movement and mother love are one, Rosa Parritt. Don makes this point repeatedly to Larry, the father figure, throughout the play, and Larry does not deny it. "To hear her talk sometimes, you'd think she was the Movement," Don tells Larry in act one. In act two he tells him that "She was always getting the Movement mixed up with herself," and in act three, "The Movement is her life." Don's betrayal of the Movement is the oedipal revenge of a rejected son. As a "free Anarchist," Rosa Parritt was determinedly promiscuous by principle. But Don, like so many other young O'Neill men, cannot reconcile sex and motherhood: whores are defilement and mothers are purity, of that he is certain. Rosa's behavior "made home a lousy place. . . . It was like living in a whorehouse" (act 2). Sharing this reaction with Don is the rejected lover, Larry, who also left Rosa and the Movement, in part, because he did not like living with a whore. It is a great, ironical touch of O'Neill's to have the desperately driven oedipal son come to enlist the father's aid in punishing him for revenging himself against their mutual rival.

Don's life, thus, is finished: for the want of a mother the ideal was lost. Here at this incipient corner of his emotional growth, love failed to enter. And once again the Movement, by sacrificing the one for the many, the short for the long, has spawned violence. By choosing to love all mankind, Rosa has lost the loving of her own son. When Don indicts his mother's hardness of purpose by saying "There's nothing soft or sentimental about Mother" (act 1), he indicts the whole of the grand Anarchist Movement and all such mass nostrums. One can either grow up or grow down, O'Neill says, and this is the way to grow down. Don betrayed his betrayers, Rosa and the Movement, because they acted to unfetter him and leave him alone in the abyss.

The Movement is too humanitarian for Hugo, not humanitarian enough for Don, but too much of both for the Hamlet-like tragic hero of the play, Larry Slade. Early in the play he admits to the contemplative flaw: "I was born condemned to be one of those who has to see all sides of a question. When you're damned like that, the questions multiply for you until in the end it's all question and no answer" (act 1). Larry feels too deeply to act. And because he is a more fully evolved being than most, he is closer to engulfment. His home is the tenuous, shifting no-man's-land between disillusion and nightmare. Objective reality is possible for him, but seemingly too horrible even to consider. Larry's sense of pity derives from his dormant Christianity, while his dejection derives from the failure of the Movement.

At a conscious level, Larry left the Movement, which to him represented mankind's movement toward ideal lifedom, because of his frustration over the slow progress, and because he became aware of the many inevitable pitfalls to which Movers are susceptible. Material greed is the principal one, as it is in all of O'Neill's plays. At the outset of *Iceman*, Larry makes this part of his motives clear: "I'm through with the Movement long since. I saw men didn't want to be saved from themselves, for that would mean they'd have to give up greed, and they'll never pay that price for liberty" (act 1). Just a little later in act one, Larry tells Don of the pervasive destruction of soul-encroaching greed to mankind as a whole: "The material the free society must be constructed from is men themselves and you can't build a marble temple out of a mixture of mud and manure. When man's soul isn't a sow's ear, it will be time enough to dream of silk purses." That "When," notice, is conditional. It is Larry's (and perhaps O'Neill's) last possible straw to clutch. *When* certain changes have been made in some distant future, man may attain enough fullness of soul to tackle the dilemma of community life. Until then reform is wasted; indeed, Movements are likely to produce more hate than love. Man's loving side, as O'Neill tried to say in *Days without End*, is in constant danger of being overtaken by his hating side.

Without doubt, misdirected love is at the heart of the Movement's dissolution; it can be seen not only in the Rosa-Don betrayals, but just as disastrously in the Rosa-Larry sexual breakup. Rosa's masculine love of freedom destroyed her feminine freedom of love. In this sense, her promiscuity only chained her to a harsh, unwieldy anarchy. Larry, for his part, was not able to absorb the sudden insistence that sexual reform be placed ahead of the love of a man and a woman. Because he thought Rosa put love of mankind above love of man, Larry left her and the Movement. In *Iceman* he still feels the loss of that part of the ideal, as does Rosa, for she still saves his letters. As always, O'Neill makes it clear that the blame belongs to the female. The damage that Rosa does is immense; regeneration is blocked and the future negated. And the loss of love kills Don and half-kills Larry.

The constricting Movement is thus thrice lovelorn: love of friend (Hugo), flesh (Don), and lover (Larry). The loss causes all three to hate: Hugo hates the proletariat, Don hates his mother, and Larry hates himself. All are permanently damaged and inexorably given over to despair. And this major theme of unrecoupable love is echoed throughout the play, as Edwin Engel noticed. To Engel, *Iceman* is O'Neill's unmasking of love:

> Love is an illusion, and all women are bitches or whores. Palpable and undisguised symbols of this truth are the three prostitutes, the only women to appear on the stage. Yet the presence of four others is felt: Hickey's wife, Evelyn; Parritt's mother, Rosa; Hope's wife, Bessie; Jimmie Cameron's wife, Marjorie.

Lack of love, mother love, is the killer of Don; of that we may be certain. But women are not clearly the killers in all of the barroom cases. Jimmy Cameron (Tomorrow), for instance, turned to booze and pipe dreams even before his wife Marjorie began going out with other men. Eventually, Jimmy admits that his wife's adultery was only an excuse: "I discovered early in life that living frightened me when I was sober" (act 3). Inability to go through the door of disillusion is what kills Jimmy and most of the others. Love might sustain one on the way through that abyss, but only possibly. In *Iceman*, we have no successful case. Larry and Rosa's one-time love and Don's and Hickey's ambivalence towards their love objects suggest the possibility, but not the probability. Spiritual strength, soulness, is needed for that. The Movement lacks soul. It symbolizes one of the many means by which modern man, to his great cost, dehumanizes himself.

The Movement, however, is but one-half of modern man's dilemma; his religious failure is the other. The hard sell evangelism of the Hickeys of the world blights faith just as surely as the Movement blights love. And love and faith are the two prime components of the O'Neill soul. In all his plays the main task is to make these two into one, or, failing this, expose that which prevents the union. It is thus in irony that the Movement is often spoken of as a faith (Hugo "rotted ten years in prison for his faith") (act 2), and Hickey's zeal called a movement ("He's started a movement that'll blow up the world!") (act 2).

Just as Don has absorbed the worst of the Movement, so Hickey has absorbed the worst of religion. The son of a small town Hoosier minister, himself a hardware salesman, Hickey is the false Messiah, as many explicators have pointed out. The pressure of his pitch for a sudden and complete facing up to life only annihilates the feeble pipe dreams by which the "hicks" of mankind live, leaving only the peaceless certainty of death in their place. Motivated by hate, but believing that he is full of love, Hickey brings with him the naked threat of reality. To all those who cannot survive a confrontation with the abyss, and there turn out to be none in *Iceman* who can, the spiritual salesman is the iceman of death. The birthday party that Hickey stages for Harry Hope ironically imitates Leonardo da Vinci's "Last Supper," with Hickey as Christ and the twelve derelicts as his disciples. But the disciples of the self-appointed Christ do not learn faith-love from him; instead, each at his moment of truth turns on Hickey with despair-hate. Throughout the play, it is Hope who most reveals the destructive effects of Hickey's layer-peeling. As Hickey increases the verve of his appeal to him, urging him to take that walk around the ward that he has deferred for twenty years, Hope's good-natured, "without malice" temperament begins to turn into fearful hatred. By the time he actually steps out into the street, he does so "in a sudden fury, his voice trembling with hatred" (act 3). Just as the Movement led to mass violence and hatred, as seen in the bombings on the West Coast, so Hickey's messianic complex led him to kill his wife and to incur the wrath of his fellow man.

In the end, even Hickey senses that his attempt to bring cold-sober reality to Hope's people has been futile. "It was a waste of time coming here" (act 4), he admits to Everychorus just before being led away to prison by Moran (*mors*, death) and Lieb (love). Just before this crushing acknowledgment, Hickey gives up his attempts to convert the men of

Hope. In response to the immediate pressure of Hope's exploding resentment, he agrees to put up a "bluff" that he was insane at the time he killed Evelyn and in everything he has said and done in the barroom since. Eric Bentley suggests that the personal love-hate problem between Hickey and Hope is the main cause of Hickey's putting on his "antic disposition," but this must be extended. Hickey never reaches conscious awareness that his evangelism has been wholly destructive; he has not Larry's gift of contemplation. Hickey does *sense,* however, that his own need, and thus mankind's need, for Hope is far more fundamental than his messianic impulse. He sees instinctively that an unconverted Hope, like an uncommitted Don Parritt, is better than a converted and committed hate. Hickey is not able to put his own hate for Evelyn and Hope's hate together, but the audience can. We discover what we knew, that to judge others without having judged ourselves, or without having judged ourselves *accurately,* is both hate-induced and hate-inducing. Hickey can tell us no more, for he cannot take his own death-loving medicine. His only real experience, his hate for Evelyn, was merely an attempt to release his own guilt. Small wonder that, out of charity, he transferred this aim to others, and set out to free all mankind. Like all of the other bums save one, Larry Slade with the intellect, Hickey learns only that pipe dreams must sometimes be replaced, but not pipe dreaming.

Larry Slade is the center balance in the religious theme of *Iceman,* just as he is in the Movement theme. It may be said that he is a deserter of Christianity, but he is not a confirmed one. His progress in the play is from loss of belief to momentary reacceptance to final rejection. Most of the time, as O'Neill's character description of Larry aptly states, "He stares in front of him, an expression of tired tolerance giving his face the quality of a pitying but weary priest's" (act 1). Larry is what O'Neill saw Christianity as being: old, tired, and pitying. But Larry, like modern Western man, cannot help feeling the pull of his Christian heritage, especially when the subject of death is in the air. When Hickey makes a passing jibe at Larry about that "old Big Sleep" during Hope's birthday party, "Larry starts and for a second looks superstitiously frightened" (act 2). At Hickey's announcement of Evelyn's death, Larry again has a "superstitious shrinking" (act 2). And when Larry hears the "crunching thud" of Don's body off the fire escape, "a long-forgotten faith returns to him for a moment" (act 4). Larry's typical superstitious dread is the timeworn product of his residual faith, but his Christ experience at the time of Don's suicide is, as we shall see, a purloined attempt to find Hickey's "right kind of pity."

Self-pity and sometimes pity for others, not Christian compassion, is the non-soulstate to which O'Neill's modern man is reduced. "What pity for oneself and what pity for others?" is, indeed, one wording of the central question in *Iceman*. Instead of the Greeks "Nothing in excess," modern man's motto is "Nothing of pity in excess." All of the characters in *Iceman* have pity problems; it is what unites them. Their degree of forbearance ranges all the way from Don's total self-pity to Evelyn's total selfless pity, with Larry's mixture of pity for himself and others as the standard. Don represents deprivation of love, while Evelyn suggests a surfeit of love. The lovelorn Don grew crooked and, in a moment of hate, betrayed his mother; Evelyn's excess of love caused Hickey to become twisted and, in a similar mood, to kill her. "There's a limit to the guilt you can feel" (act 4), Hickey explains, and he speaks for Don, too, who has also reached this limit. But Don and Evelyn, the two extremes of pity, are also symbolic Christian personages. Don is Judas and Evelyn is the Virgin Mary. Neither sustains life in *Iceman*. Whereas Judas is a negative and Mary a positive force in the Bible, both are negative in *Iceman,* as befits O'Neill's modern world. As Larry puts it, "Honor or dishonor, *faith or treachery* are nothing to me but the opposites of the same stupidity which is ruler and king of life, and in the end they rot into dust in the same grave" (act 2, my italics). Don is not evil and Evelyn is not good; both are merely pitiful. In a sense, Evelyn dies from lack of pity for herself and Don dies for lack of pity for others. The two taken together suggest that pity, to be viable at all, must be balanced between "right" self-pity and "right" pity for others. What is missing in both, of course, is compassion, the willingness to act individually in support of the need to alleviate suffering. As in the other major motifs, this theme of "What price compassion?" is worked out in the tragic hero of *Iceman*, Larry Slade.

Larry is our pity pilgrim, the remnant of Christian man reduced from compassionate commitment to passive pity. Larry pities himself and everyone else, and tries to believe that he is through with active life by assuming the role of "grandstand foolosopher." Until his moment of truth at the end of the play, it is his pipe dream that positive action is not possible in the contemporary world. He retired from the Movement because of the stubborn greed he saw in man and because he lost his faith in love, Rosa. Early in the play, however, it becomes clear that Larry has not lost his humanitarian concern, but that he is in imminent danger of seeing it disintegrate into the distorted, useless self-pity of Hugo. Larry is falling out of life, dying to despair. It is at this point that the revivalist, Hickey, enters.

Hickey, as we eventually learn, by a pipe dream-induced misreading of his own experience completely rejects passive pity and preaches self-help through redemption. He misinterpreted his motive for killing Evelyn. If he *had* done it to "give her peace and free her from the misery of loving" him (act 4) that would have been a loving, mankind-sustaining act. He did not, though. At the taut end of his tethered guilt, he discovered that he hated her. After killing her, as he finally confesses in act 4, he had said, "Well, you know what you can do with your pipe dream now, you damned bitch!" The horror of Hickey's confession lies in his admission that the "not-self" in life can neither be mitigated nor endured, that the infringement of the outer force is both irreconcilable and irreparable. In a sense, one must convert or suffer conversion from others. Hickey chose to become a proselytizer because Evelyn's difference made his loveless self feel guilty. "The sting of conscience teaches one to sting," said O'Neill's preacher, Nietzsche, in *Thus Spake Zarathustra*.

Hickey would rend *some* self-deceit, but not all, and Larry is his one convert. Hickey assigns Larry the task of destroying self-pity (Don). In a key scene between the deluded preacher and the pity pilgrims, Hickey defines his idea of Right Pity:

> Of course, I have pity. But now I've seen the light, it isn't my old kind of pity—the kind yours is. It isn't the kind that lets itself off easy by encouraging some poor guy to go on kidding himself with a lie—that kind leaves the poor slob worse off because it makes him feel guiltier than ever—the kind that makes his lying hopes nag at him and reproach him until he's a rotten skunk in his own eyes. I know all about that kind of pity. I've had a bellyful of it in my time, and it's all wrong! (With a salesman's persuasiveness) No, sir. The kind of pity I feel now is after final results that will really save the poor guy, and make him contented with what he is, and quit battling himself, and find peace for the rest of his life.
>
> (Act 2)

Although he has not followed this philosophy, Hickey believes what he says, that Right Pity comes from responsible, compassionate action. It is this definition of pity that Larry eventually accepts completely when he acts to order Don out of life. And just as Hickey was wrong in his hate-induced murder of Evelyn, so Larry is similarly wrong in his compulsion for "final results" with Don. The difference between them is the difference between tragedy and pathos—Larry knows it.

From the first, Larry tries to avoid his decision-making responsibility with Don. An act of any kind, he feels, would be regressive; it would return him to a previous, simpler state of existence. It is Larry's illusion that he is out of life by choice, and that to choose to return is both useless and self-destructive. "Look out how you try to taunt me back into life," Larry warns Don. "I might remember the thing they call justice there, and the punishment for—" (act 2). It is precisely this expiation of guilt through punishment that Don wants and that the messianic Hickey wishes to arrange. Don begs for fatherly guidance from both Larry the priest and Larry the sire, and Hickey prods Larry to settle with Don in order to get Larry out of his "grandstand bluff."

Just before the explosion of that pent-up guilt in act 4, however, Hickey's seemingly benevolent motives for dealing with Don turn to hate, just as they had with Evelyn. When Don, the most repugnant character ever created by O'Neill, taunts both Larry and Hickey with the glee of his betrayal of Rosa, Hickey is "disturbed" and says *with a movement of repulsion*: I wish you'd get rid of that bastard, Larry. I can't have him pretending there's something in common between him and me. It's what's in your heart that counts. There was love in my heart, not hate." Hickey is, of course, self-deluded. There was, and is, hate in his heart, too. Both Hickey and Don suffer from their ambivalence.

In what follows, surely one of the greatest scenes in modern drama, Larry begins by also taking this wrong path towards release. He tries to deal with Don through Hickey's hate. His face is "*convulsed with detestation. His quivering voice has a condemning command in it:* Go! Get the hell out of life, God damn you, before I choke it out of you! Go up—!'" Larry is leaving his grandstand, all right, but out of hate. Surprisingly, Don is immediately relieved and immensely grateful to Larry. "I just wanted to be sure," Don says humbly. The irony is that he becomes "sure" by arousing Larry's hate, an emotionally true process that he understands and trusts. Hate itself has its positive side, and not just with Don and Hickey. Larry was impelled by hate, but it led to a compassionate act, and transformed even him, at least momentarily. He now pleads with Don: "Go, for the love of Christ, you mad tortured bastard, for your own sake!" Don answers with awed, pious fumblings to the newly ascended Christ of the piece: "Jesus, Larry, thanks. That's kind. I knew you were the only one who could understand my side of it." For an instant, Larry is Christ, or, as in the Mass, Christ is present in Larry. His kindness is the selfless mercy of Christ, and he is truly the only one who can understand the betrayal of a Judas. Hickey was the false Christ, but here, for this small moment, Larry becomes the true Savior. When Don rushes out to jump off the fire escape, it is as a confessed man.

All during Larry's tense wait for the suicide, he wavers between his superstitious dread and his compassion. Hugo observes him and rightly predicts, "Soon comes the Day of Judgment!" When Larry finally hears the sound of Don's body land on the street outside, he says "in a whisper of horrified pity: Poor devil! (*A long-forgotten faith returns to him for a moment and he mumbles*) God rest his soul in peace!" Larry is now at his highest moment of awareness. He has returned to his lost faith, and he can pray for man. But Larry is also at a final point of no return. It is here that he must go over to death or come back to life. It is a problem of emotional choice, not of the will, as it always is in O'Neill's plays. What are the emotional attractions and consequences of an action, any action? And here it should be added that there is no question of whether or not O'Neill introduced "concealed blasphemies in his play" in the Christ symbolism, nor of the possibility that he laughed "in secret at the critics who supposed that he had written a compassionate play in *The Iceman Cometh*," as Cyrus Day speculated [elsewhere]. Larry is truly at his ultimate anguish, and his anguish is that of god-losing modern man, according to O'Neill, caught between Joyce's two worlds.

Immediately after this mystic experience, Larry "opens his eyes" in what is a symbolic awakening and says to himself with the "bitter self-derision" of a totally disillusioned man:

> Ah, the damned pity—the wrong kind, as Hickey said! Be God, there's no hope! I'll never be a success in the grandstand—or anywhere else! Life is too much for me! I'll be a weak fool looking with pity at the two sides of everything till the day I die! (*With an intense bitter sincerity*) May that day come soon! (*He pauses startledly, surprised at himself—then with a sardonic grin*) Be God, I'm the only real convert to death Hickey made here. From the bottom of my coward's heart I mean that now.

Larry is dead, as the final stage direction in the play illustrates; "Larry stares in front of him, oblivious to their racket." In the aftermath of his emotional distillation, he knows that Hickey's "Right Pity" is a failure. His end-stopped past, the Movement and Rosa, had warned Larry against such sudden, violent emancipations, but Hickey's drumming din and Don's piteous plight drew him back to active life. Don's release does not relieve

Larry, as he so had hoped; it ends him. Here, at the most nihilistic point in modern drama, Larry yields to the forces of nothingness. The two sides of everything have destroyed him. He can no longer live the lie of a pipe dream of disillusionment, for he knows now that reality is disillusion. Nor can he live in that reality, for he has only life-denying despair left in him. His "Be God, there's no hope" might well be changed to "*Play* God and there's *still* no hope!" Even when modern man plays God out of love of man, as in Larry's case, he does so only to compensate for his inner ache, his fear of tragic futility, of death. The final irony of Larry's religious failure is that his Christ-act had effect on Don, on betrayal, but not on himself. He is left empty.

Larry's earlier observation, "When man's soul isn't a sow's ear, it will be time enough to dream of silk purses" (act 1), has come home to roost. If Larry is the best of man, a contemplative coward, that still isn't much good. But just as surely, if there is to be a better man, he must come out of Larry. He cannot come from Rosa who now is going to play the "great incorruptible Mother of the Revolution" in prison and say of her son, "I'm glad he's dead!" (act 4). Nor can best man spring from Hickey, the self-proclaimed lunatic. Best man must be nurtured from that still unconquerable part of the Larry Slade who concludes with a "sardonic grin" on his face: "Be God, I'm the only real convert to death Hickey made here." Of such is modern tragedy; not death-defying, but self-defying.

TRAVIS BOGARD

The Historian: Mourning Becomes Electra and Ah, Wilderness!

During the period of its composition, O'Neill spoke less about *Mourning Becomes Electra* than he had about any other play he had composed up to that time, with the single exception of *Desire under the Elms*. The pairing is perhaps a significant one, for the two plays have much in common— their use of Greek myths as a narrative base, their New England scene, the intense psychological focus of the subject matter, their historical perspective, their primary realism which avoids all the trappings of the Art Theatre and their inner conviction which in no little measure anticipates the mood of the late plays. Compared to the theological romances which surrounded them, the quality of these two plays is one of intense, even recessive concentration, bearing the quality of a private statement. O'Neill held them both close to his chest during their creation, as if he were unwilling to release them to the theatrical world until there was nothing more he was able to do with them.

O'Neill's mention of *Mourning Becomes Electra* in letters, even to his most intimate friends, is vague and general. To Joseph Wood Krutch on July 27, 1929, he wrote of the necessity for selecting a big subject for his art, and described his current project as one of the biggest ever attempted in modern drama, comparing it to plays by the Greeks and the Elizabethans in its possibilities. In the same letter he cried, "'Oh for a language to write drama in! For a speech that is dramatic and not just conversation. I'm so strait jacketed by writing in terms of talk. I'm so fed up with the dodge-question of dialect. But where to find that language?" The cry presents the problem of matching the Greek theme with an appropriate dialogue—a problem which was to dog him after the production of the play. But nothing more is said of the nature of the work.

A similar statement to Benjamin de Casseres, to whom he wrote ordinarily with great candor, occurs in a letter dated April 20, 1930. He had, he said, finished the first draft of his new work, but he stated only that he worked on it harder than on any of his other plays. He had no idea when it would be ready for production. Not until August 23, 1930, did he reveal the subject matter in a letter to Manuel Komroff, and then his bare account—that it is a retelling of the Orestes story laid in New England at the close of the Civil War, that it is a "psychological drama of lust" and that it has more complicated relationships than any Greek treatment—was sent *"in strictest confidence."*

His secrecy and his refusal to predict a probable production season for the work suggests that he was conscientiously attempting to avoid the mistakes he made with *Dynamo*, which he let out of his hands before it was ready, and of which he talked too freely before its production. Now, living in France, under the shelter of his new marriage, he could seek to fulfill himself, taking all the time he needed, not going off, as he phrased it, "half-cocked," but struggling to achieve "a mature outlook as an artist." *Mourning Becomes Electra* was the first product of what he had termed "a complete upheaval, a total revaluing of all my old values." The luxury of time for visions and revisions came about in part because O'Neill, after the success of *Strange Interlude* was in a good financial position, and in part because he was under no necessity of providing plays for a hungry theatre. The Theatre Guild could easily afford to wait and was as committed to O'Neill as he was to it. Thus the work proceeded slowly, arduously. Between November, 1929, and August, 1930, he told Komroff, he had spent 225 working days on the script, and it was then by no means completed. His plans for vacations in order to gain a perspective were frustrated by the intensity of his application to the task. Nothing, it seems true, existed in his life except the security of his marriage and his work.

Although he closed a circle of silence around the script, the composition of the play is better documented than most by a work diary he kept during the period of its creation. Published extracts from the diary date from spring, 1926, and continue through September, 1931, as he worked on the galley proofs shortly before the play was produced.

The first entry asks whether it is possible to get a "modern psychological approximation of Greek sense of fate" into a play intended to move an audience which no longer believes in supernatural retribution. Perhaps the

Electra story or that of Medea would serve? A gap of two and a half years follows the original entry, and then in October, 1928, while on the Arabian Sea bound for China, he begins again on his "Greek tragedy plot idea," and appears to have settled on "Electra and family" as being "psychologically most interesting—most comprehensive intense basic human interrelationships." By November, the idea has taken firmer hold, and he notes that it will be important to give Electra a tragic ending worthy of her. With that he has found his area of contribution. "Why did the chain of fated crime and retribution ignore her mother's murderess?—a weakness in what remains to us of Greek tragedy that there is no play about Electra's life after the murder of Clytemnestra. Surely it possesses as imaginative tragic possibilities as any of their plots!" O'Neill's addition to the story, then, will be the punishment of Electra who "has too much tragic fate within her soul" to be allowed to slip from heroic legend into "undramatic married banality." With this definition of central narrative focus, he is ready to begin.

Other details followed slowly. By April, 1929, he had decided to set the story in an American historical setting, always provided that it remain a "modern psychological drama." The story needs time and distance, but the period is to be only a mask over the "drama of hidden life forces—fate— behind lives of characters." He recognizes that the Civil War with its heroic, even epic scale is the best possible period, permitting the desired modernity, yet also providing the time and distance essential to the tragic legend.

Quickly, thereafter, details of setting and time are sketched in: New England and the Puritan sense of retribution, the house that resembles with total architectural and thematic justification a Greek temple. He lists his departures from the Greek story at length in notes on the relationships of the characters to one another. At the end of the entry which conveys a sense of excited discovery, he is concerned to stress family resemblances, "as visible sign of the family fate," and he adds, "use masks (?)." By May the names of the characters are in order, developed on a simple alliterative scheme with the Greek names, and he has found his title, using "Becomes" in the sense of "befits": "that is ... it befits—it becomes Electra to mourn—it is her fate—also, in usual sense (made ironical here), mourning (black) is becoming to her—it is the only color that becomes her destiny." The play's structure is clear, a trilogy, and he has the titles of the first and third plays, *The Homecoming* and *The Haunted*. He begins on the scenario in June, 1929, eight months after settling on the Electra story, and he has decided to write the first draft as "straight realism" in order to get the play into definitive form before worrying about the use of masks or soliloquies and asides.

The scenarios were finished by August, having raised a problem about which O'Neill was curiously bothered: how to arrange the murders so that no tedious police action would follow. The first draft was written between September, 1929, and February, 1930, and laid aside for a month. Rereading it in March, he found much of it "scrawny" but parts of it were "damned thrilling." What he had failed to provide was a "sense of fate hovering over the characters. . . . I get the feeling that more of my idea was left out of play than there is in it! In next version I must correct this at all costs—run the risk of going to other cluttered up extreme—use every means to gain added depth and scope." To get it, he determines to "use half masks and an 'Interlude' technique (combination 'Lazarus' and 'Interlude') and see what can be gotten out of that—think these will aid me to get just the right effect—must get more distance and perspective—more sense of fate—more sense of the unreal behind what we call reality which is the real reality!—the unrealistic truth wearing the mask of lying reality, that is the right feeling for this trilogy, if I can only catch it!" He writes an *aide-memoire* about the dialogue in which he reminds himself not to be too faithful to the speech of the historical period, and he discusses with himself the alternation of scenes, each play to begin and end with an exterior, and to create a rhythm between interior and exterior settings in the course of each play. One scene is to break this rhythm, that on Adam Brant's ship at the center of the second play: "(this, center of whole work) emphasizing sea background of family and symbolic motive of sea as a means of escape and release." The notes continue to discuss the chorus, the development of the South Sea Island motif, the desirable "characterlessness" of Peter and Hazel, the use of the chanty "Shenandoah" and the problem of controlling melodrama in the story. The entry ends with a reiteration of the diary's constant theme: "it must, before everything, remain modern psychological play—fate springing out of the family."

Between March and July, 1930, he wrote the second draft and records his fatigue on completing it. He promises himself a vacation, but within a week he is back at work, and on rereading the second draft, he finds its use of "Interludisms" cluttering. He writes himself a warning: "always hereafter regard with suspicion hangover inclination to use 'Interlude' technique regardless—that was what principally hurt 'Dynamo,' being forced into thought-asides method which was quite alien to essential psychological form of its characters—did not ring true—only clogged up play arbitrarily with author's mannerisms. . . . 'Interlude' aside technique is special expression for special type of modern neurotic, disintegrated soul—when dealing with simple direct folk or characters of strong will and intense passions, it is superfluous showshop 'business.' " A second rereading the next day convinced him that the masks introduced wrong connotations. The play's soliloquies were also troublesome. He sought to give them a stronger connection with the masks, and thought perhaps that by arranging soliloquies in a fixed structural pattern he could make both masks and soliloquies effective. He urges himself to "try for prose with simple forceful repeating accent and rhythm which will express driving insistent compulsion of passions engendered in family past, which constitute family fate." The next day, he began to rewrite the second draft and to cut it, a process he finished on September 16, 1930. The dialogue went well, and the omission of the asides was right. Now the play was to be laid aside to gain perspective.

Only four days elapsed. By the twentieth, he was back at work. The soliloquies and masks were bad because they introduced an "obvious duality-of-character symbolism quite outside my intent in these plays." They were dropped along with the asides, and by September 21, he knew that while the second draft had been profitable in that the "Interludisms" had given him new insights, it remained to rewrite the entire play "in straight dialogue—as simple and direct and dynamic as possible—with as few words—stop doing things to these characters—let them reveal themselves." The concept of the masks he decided to keep, but now he saw that make-up could achieve the effect he wanted—that of a death-mask "suddenly being torn open by passion." What the play needed, he felt, was a stronger structural rhythm: "Repetition of the same scene—in its essential spirit, sometimes even in its exact words, but between different characters—following plays as development of fate—theme demands this repetition." And he noted, "Mannon drama takes place on a plane where outer reality is mask of true fated reality—unreal realism."

The third complete draft was started two days later, on September 23, and finished by October 15. Finally, then, he took a vacation, returning to work in mid-November, expressing himself as "fairly well satisfied" with the last script, which he reworked until January 10, 1931. The script was typed, but by February 7, he found himself dissatisfied with the last revision, and began to prune back recent additions. The revision was finished on February 20, and he went to the Canary Islands, where on March 8 he read the typed script.

In type the script looked "damned good," although it was long and some sections needed rewriting, cutting, pointing up. This work was finished by March 26, and by April 9 new typed copies were prepared and the final script sent to the Theatre Guild. In August, 1931, he read the play in galley proof, and, after a lapse of nearly four months without reading the work, he found he was moved by it and that it had "power and drive and the strange quality of unreal reality I wanted—main purpose seems to me soundly achieved—there is a feeling of fate in it, or I am a fool—a psychological approximation of the fate in the Greek tragedies on this theme—attained without benefit of the supernatural." In addition he expressed himself as pleased with its structure as a trilogy. In August and September, he worked on the galley proofs. Some matters remained to be ironed out, but, as the work diary ends, he had little more to do that could not be accomplished during rehearsals. *Mourning Becomes Electra* was at last ready for the stage.

The enormous consecutive creative effort was a staggering labor. Between May, 1929, when he wrote the scenarios, and February, 1931, when he finished the third draft, he was away from the script no more than two months and a few days. It was an expenditure of incredible strength that was to define, so far as the matter can be judged, the working habits of his mature years. The routines of ordinary life dropped away from him as he worked, and the result was very different from what had gone before.

Although the phrase "unreal realism" that runs through the diary suggests that some of the pretensions of the Art Theatre Show Shop still remained, the ruthless excision of the elements of technical exhibitionism for which he had become famous makes clear that the trilogy was truly the result of "a complete upheaval" of his old values, as he had claimed.

If further proof than that offered by the play were needed, a letter to Macgowan written on June 14, 1929, amounts to a renunciation of Art Theatre principles and of Macgowan's guidance:

> No more sets or theatrical devices as anything but unimportant background—except in the most imperatively exceptional case where organically they belong. To read *Dynamo* is to stumble continually over the sets. They're always in my way, writing and reading—and they are in the way of the dramatic action. Hereafter I write plays primarily as literature to be read—and the more simply they read, the better they will act, no matter what technique is used. *Interlude* is proof of this. I don't mean that I wouldn't use masks again in the writing if a *Lazarus* or *Brown* should demand it—but I do mean that my trend will be

to regard anything depending on director or scenic designer for collaboration to bring out its full values as suspect. *Brown & Lazarus*, of course, don't. They will always convey more to a reader's imagination than any production can give. But I'm fed up with the show shop we call a theatre in the world today and I refuse to write any more which uses it. Constructivism and such stuff is all right for directors but it's only in an author's way. At least that's the way I feel now. Greater classical simplicity, austerity combined with that utmost freedom and flexibility, that's the stuff!

The new mood represented a deliberate retrenchment, a decisive and controlled return to a point of origin, a recession of art and spirit. It was an essential change if O'Neill was to continue to write for the theatre. He had built his reputation on the work he did for the theatre of the Triumvirate. He was famous for the furious breaking of theatrical icons as he plunged toward the goals the aestheticians descried with a literal, bold directness that shocked and excited his audiences. George Jean Nathan once said that audiences were more excited by the phenomenon of O'Neill than they were by his plays. The comment is revealing and just. O'Neill was a "presence," and the première of one of his works was a national event, not quite in the category of other drama. Yet, as O'Neill disappeared into France, a new theatre, Depression-oriented and alive to social causes, emerged in the United States. It was not the kind of theatre in which O'Neill could take direct part, and it moved away from the tenets of theatrical art O'Neill had held. *Dynamo* failed and *Days without End* would not write. Both plays were marred by failing power and a serious diminishment of genuine creative energy. Hence the need for a new direction.

Once before, O'Neill had come to such a pass after committing himself to the theories of George Pierce Baker and the 47 Workshop. Then after a period of doldrums, he gripped and forcefully changed direction. When he was young, it was an easy matter, much less difficult than the change after his commitment to Macgowan. Yet his process of return was the same in both instances. He recovered from Baker's doctrine by writing *Before Breakfast* in unrelenting imitation of Strindberg, with whom Baker was unconcerned. That play was a jumping-off spot for his first serious work.

As he had done before, he turned again from the false lights he had followed, selected a model he admired and in reworking older material found once more the sources of his creative life. This time, because the commitments of the past ten years were so strong, he could not do it easily. His own habits, his imagination, his involvement with brute size and with important themes, to say nothing of the expectations of his audiences, led him by no conscious route to the source of all tragedy, the *Oresteia* of Aeschylus, and to the later plays which spun off from it. From that primal fountain, he took new life.

The act, if such a subconscious thrust can be called an act, was, like all he did, daring and even presumptuous. Yet it can be seen in a historical perspective. *Mourning Becomes Electra* takes its place in the forefront of many modern dramas based on Greek themes and written by the greatest names in the modern theatre: Giraudoux, von Hofmannsthal, Eliot, Sartre, Shaw among many others. It is part of the twentieth-century Greek revival; yet, for all this, the work emerged as the end product of private necessity. The irony presents itself: *Days without End*, a story of salvation, meant damnation for its author; whereas his study of the damned brought his own salvation as an artist.

His modern parallels for the Electra story are appropriate and unforced. The Civil War and the New England Greek-style architecture provided a satisfactory time and place for his history. The details of the relationships in the House of Atreus created the structure of the Mannon clan. The names, following the punning allusion to "Agamemnon" in Ezra Mannon, with its connotation of power and wealth, were developed by the alliterative scheme which at one time he tried to maintain in Lavinia by calling her "Elavinia." In the ancient servant of Electra he found Seth, just as Peter emerged from Pylades and Hazel from such innocents as Sophocles' Chrysothemis. In similar fashion, his chorus of gossips came naturally, if not entirely convincingly, from his source. Such details are obvious, but less so is O'Neill's remarkable fidelity to basic motifs of the myth: the presence of the sea in the Troy story finds congenial recapitulation in O'Neill's response to the sea and the islands of the South Pacific; the primitive need to honor the dishonored father, and the horrifying origin of the curse in the devouring of children is echoed in the fate of the Mannon heirs, Lavinia, Orin and Adam Brant; the sense of a haunted world, peopled with ghosts, and of men and women thrust into action by the dictates of a compulsive and destructive will and pursued by the furies of their own guilt are admirably brought into alignment with the legend. By the same token the trilogic structure parallels in its scope the cyclic evolution of the *Oresteia*.

In some thematic respects, *Mourning Becomes Electra* is closer to Euripides than to Aeschylus, owing to the Euripidean treatment, its psy-

chological interest and the incorrigible self-justifications for acts of violence in which Euripides' Electra and Clytemnestra engage. The incest
motif also has its strongest source in Euripides' *Orestes*. Nevertheless,
O'Neill has worked freely with his Greek material, and, as he noted in his
diary, in centering on Electra's destiny after the murder, he has added a
fresh increment to the legend. Certainly, as the legend moves behind the
work, pinning it to essentials, it makes the trilogy a larger play than it
would otherwise have been. It is a greater achievement than *Strange
Interlude*, and, compared with *Desire under the Elms*, where similar
legends, more deeply imbedded, heightened and generalized the story, the
Electra plays seem more insistently impressive.

The mixture of ancient and modern, Aeschylus and Freud, has tended
to obscure two important qualities of the trilogy. The first is that it is a
history play, and an excellent one. Granted that the Civil War offered a
luckily appropriate means of modernizing the post-Trojan-war period of
the legend, O'Neill has been at pains to make his image of post-war New
England faithful in spirit and fact to what it was. Without much apparent
research and with stringently economic means he has created the past: a
song, cannon shots celebrating the surrender, a few names from history,
lilacs, almost inevitably associated through Walt Whitman's elegy with the
death of Lincoln. In a letter to the Theatre Guild dated April 7, 1931, he
noted that "the dialogue is colloquial of today. The house, the period
costumes, the Civil War surface stuff, these are masks for what is really a
modern psychological drama with no true connection with that period at
all." His point is born of his drive revealed in the work diary to find a
substitute for elements of the legend and to make the play "modern," but
in fact, those qualities of his imagination that were to make him turn for
his last major works to America's historical past in order to explain its
present were already operating to make the past a reality and to show
therein an aspect of contemporary truth.

Thus, in his picture of the war, O'Neill creates unforgettable images
that seem to have in them historical truth. Sometimes the treatment is
elaborate as when Orin describes his falsely heroic charge in act 3 of *The
Homecoming*. The passage, which owes much to the anti-war literature of
the late 1920s, also recalls Stephen Crane's description of similar heroics
in *The Red Badge of Courage*. It is perhaps less a matter of what the war
really was than what men felt it to be. Crane defined a point of view
toward the past; O'Neill related it to his present. Past or present, the
sequence has imaginative authority.

In less elaborate ways, his re-creation of the past proves unexpectedly strong. For example in describing his feeling of the safety of a military encampment at night, Ezra Mannon says,

> I can't get used to home yet. It's so lonely. I've got used to the feel of camps with thousands of men around me at night—a sense of protection, maybe!

The words have no direct reference to the past, but they convey it vividly. The song "Tenting Tonight" sounds faintly in the mind, and the past awakes through the response of a character to his environment. As many who have lain awake in a barracks at night may recognize, the words are verifiable in present experience, and again the passage seems true for both past and present. O'Neill's remark that the historical images are "surface stuff" is less than accurate. Even if his emphasis is on the present, at no point does the play's modernity violate the image of the past. The two are conjoined to convey truth.

A consequence of the play's being set firmly in historical time is that the society in which the action moves is realized more fully than in any of his mature works except *Desire under the Elms*. Indeed, it surpasses the story of the Cabots in its creation of the social community surrounding the central action. The presence of that community, like the historical past, is suggested by economical means. A show curtain, painted to reveal the Mannon house surrounded by woods, orchards, gardens, with a drive curving to its door past a lawn, is in cinematic terms a long shot, giving a perspective on the close-ups to follow. As the play begins, sounds from town drift on the wind, keeping the presence of the community on the periphery of awareness. The "chorus," small town civic types—carpenters, sailors, clerks, doctors, gossips, visiting cousins, business men, ministers— convey something of the typicality of the chorus of *Lazarus Laughed*, but they are not so diagrammatically conceived as to create a symbolic unit. They only sketch what O'Neill called "the human background for the drama of the Mannons." The background is reinforced through the presence of Hazel and Peter, whose obligations to another kind of existence than that of the Mannons, is always present; they have parents they respect and places to go other than the central house. Finally, through Adam Brant, the world outside is brought into the play, and through him, the action is briefly shifted from its focal center to his ship, *Flying Trades*, anchored in the Boston harbor.

Both the historical frame and the full social context prevent the play from becoming like *Strange Interlude*, a drama that exists only in a limbo of purely personal emotions. The fact has important consequences. Lavinia's final act is strong in part because she lives in an inhabited world. Unlike the Hairy Ape, she is not driven out by faceless voices. Her needs are created by the society she inhabits, and because her world has meaning, her self-inflicted punishment, a rejection of that world, gains significance, if not universality. Much the same may be said of the initial isolation of the Mannons.

Legend, its parallel in history, and a fullness of social framework—each contributes new value to the play. To this list must be added the extensive use of Freudian psychology. O'Neill denied any obligation to Freud. He was irritated when critics saw Freudian patterns in *Desire under the Elms*, and, after Barrett Clark had objected to what he felt was the too explicit Freudianism of the trilogy, he replied in aggrieved tones,

> I find fault with critics [who] read too damn much Freud into stuff that could very well have been written exactly as is before psychoanalysis was ever heard of. . . . After all, every human complication of love and hate in my trilogy is as old as literature, and the interpretations I suggest are such as might have occurred to any author in any time with a deep curiosity about the underlying motives that actuate human interrelationships in the family. In short, I think I know enough about men and women to have written *Mourning Becomes Electra* almost exactly as it is if I had never heard of Freud, Jung or the others. . . . I am no deep student of psychoanalysis. As far as I can remember, of all the books written by Freud, Jung, etc., I have read only four, and Jung is the only one of the lot who interests me. Some of his suggestions I find extraordinarily illuminating in the light of my own experience with hidden human motives.

Freud, however, had been part of his knowledge since at least the early days of the Provincetown Players, when Cook and his wife had written a satire on the pretensions of Freudian cultists, called *Suppressed Desires*. More importantly in 1926, he had taken part as a subject in Dr. G. V. Hamilton's research into marital problems, and at the conclusion had received a brief "psychoanalytic" counseling from Hamilton. The sessions, which lasted only six weeks, were conducted in the traditional manner of Freudian analysis, with the patient on a black leather couch. Although the principal matter of concern was to put an end to O'Neill's excessive drinking, O'Neill told Macgowan that he had learned he was suffering

from an Oedipus complex. The Freudian world was professionally opened
to him through Hamilton.

Hamilton's survey, *A Research in Marriage*, was published in 1929,
the year O'Neill began serious work on *Mourning Becomes Electra*. Perhaps more readily available to him, and certainly more readable, was a
popular book derived from the same series of interviews and written, in
collaboration with Hamilton, by Kenneth Macgowan, who like O'Neill
had offered himself as a subject for the interviews. *What Is Wrong with
Marriage*, also published in 1929, is essentially Macgowan's book. In a
preface, Hamilton acknowledges that Macgowan had made himself a
member of the research team, and that he had contributed greatly to the
analysis of the materials for their human, rather than for their clinical
value.

Chapter 9 of Macgowan's book is titled "Oedipus Rex"; chapter 10 is
"The Tragedy of Electra." Macgowan defines the Oedipus complex in
these terms:

> You get a mother complex, in most cases, because your mother
> loved your father too little and loved you too much. It was as
> though she said at your birth: "I don't love my husband, so I'm
> going to concentrate all my affection on this man-child of
> mine." . . . The kind of mother who creates this complex—
> which Freud named for the Greek king Oedipus who unwit-
> tingly killed his father and married his mother—not only develops
> too great a love for her in her son. She goes on cultivating this
> abnormal fervor, and dominating his life . . . so tenaciously
> that often he cannot look on any other woman with longing—or
> at any rate with enough longing to make him break his chains.

A little later, he speaks of the son's reaction to the taboo of incest as he
feels sexual stirrings toward his mother, and of his attempt to find as a
mate a woman who is either physically or temperamentally like his mother.

Somewhat less at ease in his analysis of the Electra complex, Macgowan
recognizes that there is no term in English such as "father's girl" which
carries connotations similar to "mother's boy." Without formally defining
the complex, he notes that if a mother continually belittles her husband in
the eyes of his daughter, thus destroying the child's image of her father,
not only will the child be unable to marry happily, but "The consequences
are likely to follow through a century." He narrates the story of a family
whose great-great-grandmother ridiculed her husband before her daughter,

and describes its consequences in similar patterns of behavior and similar unhappy marriages through several generations. "Here, indeed," he concludes, "were the sins of the mother visited upon the children even unto the fourth and fifth generations."

While there is no evidence that O'Neill read Macgowan's book, the probability is that his own participation in the research, the fact of his divorce and new marriage, together with his continuing friendship with Macgowan, led him to the work. The matter is of no great concern, for much of what was in the book undoubtedly was discussed at length.

O'Neill at moments comes very close to Macgowan's simplifications, as when Mannon says to Lavinia, "I want you to remain my little girl—for a while longer at least," or when he tells Christine, "I tried not to hate Orin. I turned to Vinnie, but a daughter's not a wife." O'Neill is right in asserting that as a dramatist, and therefore presumably something of a student of human nature, he will necessarily see patterns that reflect Freudian truths. Yet this explanation, while it satisfies for Shakespeare and for Sophocles, does not quite relieve O'Neill of indebtedness to psychoanalytic theory, which loomed large in his life in the years immediately preceding the writing of the trilogy. Hamilton and Macgowan at least brought Freud well into his range of vision, and, perhaps unconsciously, he permitted a certain clinical definition of human relationships to creep into the play, as for example Christine's line to her daughter, "You've tried to become the wife of your father and the mother of Orin! You've always schemed to steal my place!"

To write "a play containing a modern psychological approximation of the Greek sense of fate" caused O'Neill to substitute Freud for Apollo. The consequences to the trilogy were curious. O'Neill relentlessly analyzes the lives of five persons at the center of his drama. While Peter, Hazel and the townspeople are deliberately characterized by purely external means, and Seth is left on the edges of the action, Lavinia, Christine, Orin, Ezra and Adam are placed in a crucible. They are concerned with nothing but themselves, and even that concern is limited to the psycho-sexual problems which they all fatally share. The psychoanalytic approach makes such concentration possible, perhaps inevitable, and it is extraordinary that a play of this length, with so small a cast and so little variety of subject matter, can hold an audience for the length of such remorseless investigation. That it works is because, with the psychoanalytic lead, O'Neill provides an essentially *purgative* action. Whereas nothing happened to Nina Leeds, much happens to the Mannons. They discover, they grow, and they change; and what happens to them is therapeutic as psychoanalysis is therapeutic.

For example, when Ezra Mannon returns from the war, he sits with Christine on the steps of the house. He tells her of his war experiences, of his longing for her, of his hope for a better marriage in a long quasi-soliloquy similar in situation and emotional content to that which Ephraim speaks to Abbie. As a scene it is among the most effective moments of the play, but what is perhaps most noteworthy about it is that Ezra, although he speaks to Christine as his wife, also asks of her the services a patient might ask of an analyst. He cannot look at her and asks her to shut her eyes so that she may hear him neutrally, dispassionately, as a psychiatrist might, and his words move in a free association around the pivots of loneliness and desire. It comes to nothing; she will not help him or try to understand. Even so, his attempt to purge himself by speaking his truth is a way of finding release from his interior torment.

Orin's long written confession, which relates the history of the Mannons' crimes, has something of the same motivation—the psychoanalysis of a family which may lead to purgation. He tells Lavinia, "I've tried to trace to its secret hiding place in the Mannon past the evil destiny behind our lives. I thought if I could see clearly in the past I might be able to foretell what fate is in store for us." He has gone with Lavinia to the Islands that she might purge herself of her repressions and her sense of guilt, and he has come home to purge himself. Lavinia says, "You told me that if you could come home and face your ghosts, you knew you could rid yourself forever of your silly guilt about the past." At the play's climax, when Orin attempts to force his sister to the inevitable act of incest, the scene takes on something of the quality of a classic recognition scene. Orin, the course of his self-discovery completed, loves his sister who is his mother, the ghost of the mother of Adam Brant, Marie Brantôme, and also "some stranger with the same beautiful hair—" and, although his attempted seduction dies in its own disgust, it wrings from him the final plea for purgation: "Vinnie! For the love of God, let's go now and confess and pay the penalty for Mother's murder, and find peace together!" A similar realization that peace can be obtained only through payment comes to Lavinia when, crying out to Peter to love her, she calls him by Brant's name, "Want me! Take me, Adam!" As O'Neill insists, she is betrayed by her own subconscious, and recognizing its truth forswears love in her lifetime.

The course of purgative action, concentrated on the raising and recognition of submerged truths, while it can be paralleled in Greek, and Elizabethan tragedy, is, if only by virtue of its concentrated and psychoanalytic phrasing, given a "modern" quality. Macgowan, in *What Is Wrong with Marriage*, had said that men with Oedipal complexes seek to marry women like their mothers, and added that they will have a chance to be happy if the woman is physically like the mother. He does not hold out the same hope for women with "Electra complexes," although he recognizes that they will attempt to find happiness by marrying men like their fathers. O'Neill, translating the theories into a specifically incestuous context, sees in them a twisted thrusting for happiness and for a purge that at best kills desire.

In the course of the action his characters find no peace nor adjustment; the long analysis they undergo brings no satisfaction. That this is so is because O'Neill, while accepting modern psychoanalytic theory, still holds to the idea of crime and punishment that he inherited from the source in legend. In tragedy, human crime is punished by the Gods who control human destiny. A divinity shapes the end. O'Neill understands that psychoanalysis can mean an end to repression, and he causes all the Mannons to seek such an end, but he does not permit purgation to occur. Relying heavily on the Calvinistic traditions of the New England Puritan culture, his final view of the Mannons is as a dynasty bound as if by a divine edict to its destiny. "Bound" is the operative word in Seth's chanty "Shenandoah," and the repressions of Puritanism are constantly recalled through the presence of the spying townspeople, through the house and the ancestral portraits, and through the longings of all the Mannons for a different condition: for flowers, for the freedom of the sea, for the Blessed Islands. Yet they are bound as if they were in fact controlled by an angry God. The tangled web of love and lust in which they struggle is called an "evil destiny" that shapes their lives. Macgowan had spoken of a similar curse brought to families whose women had "Electra complexes," but O'Neill makes of the complex more than a psychological problem, by causing it to lead as the course of destiny in the *Oresteia* leads toward judgment, punishment, expiation of crime. O'Neill is careful to avoid significant reference to any deity as an agent of fate. Constantly the play is redirected from thoughts of God toward human responsibility. When Hazel speaks of God's forgiving Lavinia, Lavinia replies, "I'm not asking God or anybody for forgiveness. I forgive myself!" In the same spirit, she judges, condemns and punishes herself. In this, however, she acts as her own "God," rather than as her own psychoanalyst. The promise of purgation offered by psychoanalysis is finally vitiated by the drive toward self-inflicted punishment. For all its Freudian modernity, the action is controlled by the dead decrees of Olympus.

The deliberate elimination of the Gods is perhaps the clearest sign of

O'Neill's determination to make of his version of the Electra myth an uncharacteristic kind of play. In the context of his other plays written in the twenties, it is an altogether startling phenomenon. His theological plays for the Art Theatre had all been concerned with what O'Neill called the "Big Theme," the quest for God or a God substitute. Now the Gods are gone except for the atavistic traces they have left in the basic legend. What is more, no one seeks them: the motif of the questing dreamer is notable by its sudden absence. Such religious concern as is in the play is a matter of historical place, a part of the background, but not a part of the play's thematic center. And no one in this study is touched with poetry. O'Neill has shucked off all his most characteristic thematic material as he turns toward a new kind of study. Except for *Days without End*, he never returned to the old ways.

In place of former concerns new images arose and a new concept of human destiny emerged. In what O'Neill in his work diary called the "center of the whole work," the scene on Adam Brant's ship which comprises act 4 of the second play, *The Hunted*, certain elements of the new direction can be examined. Here, for a moment, O'Neill returns to the mood and manner of his early sea plays, but it is a faded image he creates. The scene reveals the afterdeck and, later, the cabin of Brant's clipper ship, *Flying Trades*, at anchor in Boston. Moonlight silhouettes the rigging, and from a neighboring ship the chanty "Shenandoah" drifts over the water. On the dock sits an old, drunken chantyman whom O'Neill describes in terms reminiscent of his former poet-hero: *"he has a weak mouth, his big round blue eyes are bloodshot, dreamy and drunken. But there is something romantic, a queer troubadour-of-the-sea quality about him."* Now, the poet, formerly O'Neill's constant hero, is old and useless, an insignificant figure on the edge of tragedy, as if Hamlet had become the Hell-Porter in *Macbeth*. He sings a chorus of "Shenandoah" and drunkenly laments the loss of his cash. Adam Brant, from the deck, orders him to keep quiet. They talk, the chantyman bragging of his ability to bring a crew into working order with his singing. He laments the coming of steam to ships and the death of the old days. With an unconscious word of prophecy, he says lugubriously, "Everything is dyin'! Abe Lincoln is dead. I used to ship on the Mannon packets an' I seed in the paper where Ezra Mannon was dead!" He praises Adam's ship, and then drunkenly disappears singing the chanty, "Hanging Johnny": "They say I hanged my mother, / Oh, hang, boys, hang!" The exit of the chantyman is the last glimpse O'Neill was to give his audiences of the protected children of the sea. Thereafter, the sea was for drowning, and even the drowned were to find no peace.

Next, Christine comes to Adam, and the scene gives way to frantic, melodramatic plotting. Christine is discovered as a murderess: "I'd planned it so carefully," she says, "but something made things happen!" The words echo Simeon Cabot's: "It's allus something'. That's the murderer," but here no sense of a directing life force is evident. Their own weaknesses, qualities Adam calls cowardice, have brought them to this desperate moment. Their loss is great. Adam must give up the ship he cares for more than the world. Earlier he has told Lavinia that to him ships are like women and that he loved them more than he had ever loved a woman. Now, he is aware that the sea is through with him. "The sea," he says, "hates a coward." What is left for them is to dream of happiness and safety on the "Blessed Isles" of the South Seas to which they plan to escape.

The image of the Blessed Isles is derived, in all probability, from the scene of the second book of *Thus Spake Zarathustra*. O'Neill, however, has made no further use of Nietzsche's philosophy, except to suggest that the islands, like the sea, like the longed-for mother, are all one, and that in them man can sink into rapture and forgetfulness. The description of the islands carry into the play some of the feeling of Dionysian ecstasy so pronounced in *Desire under the Elms*. Ephraim had said to Abbie, "Sometimes ye air the farm an' sometimes the farm be yew," and for both Orin and Adam, Christine is the embodiment of the beauty, security and peace of the earthly paradise. In *The Hunted*, Orin, telling his mother of Melville's *Typee*, speaks of a dream that came to him in a delirium. He was on Melville's islands, alone with his mother: "And yet I never saw you. . . . I only felt you all around me. The breaking of the waves was your voice. The sky was the same color as your eyes. The warm sand was like your skin. The whole island was you." To all the Mannons, even Ezra, who proposes that he and Christine take ship to find such an island, the symbol of the Islands means the same hope. Yet in the tension of the moment, Adam, at least, appears to know that the Islands are an illusion. He speaks of them thirstily:

> I can see them now—so close—and a million miles away! The warm earth in the moonlight, the trade winds rustling the coco palms, the surf on the barrier reef singing a croon in your ears like a lullabye! Aye! There's peace, and forgetfullness for us there—if we can ever find those islands now!

His last sentence denies their hope, and shortly Orin, who with Lavinia has been listening at the cabin skylight, torn with rage that Christine has shared the dream of the Islands with her lover, shoots him. Then hope stops. As he bends over the dead man, he is struck by the resemblance to his own face and anticipates his destiny: "He looks like me, too! Maybe I've committed suicide!"

The scene awakens many echoes of earlier themes and images in O'Neill's plays. The Blessed Isles lie beyond the horizon, their intimacy with nature creating in the natives a freedom from sin and a closeness to a life source. Their essence is hope, as similar concepts gave "hopeless hope" to earlier questers. Now, however, hope is not even "hopeless." No one believes in the Islands. When Lavinia and Orin go there after Christine's death, their influence transforms Lavinia's personality, turning her from her martinet, military self to a woman who is startingly like her mother but their effect is transitory. Within three days of her homecoming her repressions have returned. For Orin, there is no change whatever. The dream of the Blessed Isles is a sham, and since it is, conviction that the Islands, somehow, are set at the source of life, all feeling that the Islands are God—concepts that were urgently held in many earlier plays—are absent here. The Islands are only a refuge from a new and more urgent compulsion: to atone for guilt.

As the old dream ceases to have sustaining reality O'Neill shifts from theological and philosophical problems to ethical ones. In *Strange Interlude*, for all its emphasis on sexual behavior, nothing turned on an ethical dilemma. No blame attached to Nina for her early promiscuity; no questions beyond clinical speculation were raised with reference to her abortion or to her adultery. *Mourning Becomes Electra* is very different and very new. The only earlier hint of such concerns was in the ending of the trilogy's progenitor, *Desire under the Elms*, when Abbie and Eben accepted the guilt of their crime and their punishment. At that point, the theological implications of the play lost their strength. The lovers became their own persons, not the creatures of the forces expressed through the earth. In the trilogy, hope being gone, what is left is damnation, an acknowledgment of guilt and acceptance of the consequence: human obligation. In the shipside scene, the love, which still perhaps contains an element of hope, of Lavinia and Christine for Adam, as well as the love of Orin for Christine, is perverted and turned into hate. Guilt follows in the course of the willful actions of the guilty. Now, for the first time in O'Neill's dramas, the will begins to play a significant role. His earlier studies of obsessed men, such as Captain Keeny in *Ile* or Captain Bartlett in *Where the Cross Is Made*, were studies of madness, men who forced themselves to move beyond their limits and to deny their destiny. What is perhaps most horrifying in *Mourning Becomes Electra* is that no one, not even Orin as he comes to the point of suicide, is insane. All the actions are deliberate, the product of desire energized by ruthless purpose.

The new commitment to will and its human consequences creates for O'Neill a new set of images, both poetic and theatrical. For one, there is the image of the desolate emptiness at the bottom of the sea, expressed in Orin's words to Hazel: "The only love I can know now is the love of guilt for guilt which breeds more guilt—until you get so deep at the bottom of hell there is no lower you can sink and you rest there in peace!" The sea, which even so recently as *Dynamo*, had been thought of as a source of all life, is now hell itself.

Hell is reached through a dark doorway. When Lavinia Mannon moves to punish herself, throwing out from the house all the flowers, nailing up the shutters and turning her back on love, she marches through the door of the house that closes behind her. The image of the door, dividing life from death, sanity from madness, hope from despair, love from rejection, will become in the late plays one of O'Neill's principal images. The sound of its closing here sets the seal on Lavinia's punishment and fittingly climaxes this play of the damned.

Mourning Becomes Electra, perhaps O'Neill's most secular play, is also his least symbolic work to date. Such symbols as exist in the play, the house, for example, or the portraits, or the flowers, are all related to the human beings at the central focus. Now, none of the conflict between character and symbol that beset many of the minor works and even such major plays as *Strange Interlude* enters to plague this study of crime and retribution. There are no ambiguities; nothing is vague or suggested. The characters are drawn precisely, their story fully told, and they move toward a comprehensible and convincing destiny. Thus O'Neill returned to his point of origin, to the realistic theatre, from whence, with the single exception of *Days without End*, he never again departed. (A minor exception is the use of "Interludisms" in *More Stately Mansions*.) In this, perhaps, had he been alive to know of it, George Cram Cook might have felt a small triumph. Had he not said years earlier, in 1916, when the Provincetown Players produced *Thirst*, that O'Neill was a realist, not a writer for the Art Theatre?

The heart of an artist's mystery cannot be plucked out. Although external qualities of his imagination reveal themselves for analysis and evaluation, its generative powers hide its nature even from its possessor. It is a deep tidal current whose force and direction can be only dimly traced by the movement of surface waters. The exhausting labor of writing

Mourning Becomes Electra was a disciplining of the imagination, a prolonged, painful contraction, a brutal reining-in of the self. For a decade, justified and encouraged by the belief of the partisans of the Art Theatre, O'Neill had written romances. His friends had pointed to the romantic drama as a way for the Art Theatre to move, and for O'Neill, starting from picaresque tales that asserted the life force of the sea as a God, the development toward the extravagant climax of *Lazarus Laughed* and the anticlimax of *Dynamo* was in the context of his time as inevitable as it was self-betraying. Yet O'Neill, despite a literary taste formed on Jack London and the turn-of-the-century British poets, was no romancer. Against the continuous expansion of his dramas in length and narrative, there worked a desire to explore a small subject matter within clearly defined limits. The characteristics of his handwriting, tiny, chisled, closed, bears symbolic testimony to the fact that his writing was really dedicated to exploring a private world, the life of a few people shut in a dark room out of time. To stretch the imagination and journey to Bethany, Xanadu, Spain or mysterious tropical forests was wrong. Whatever their numerical size, O'Neill's casts are essentially small family units. The new approach to characterization that had begun with *The Great God Brown* and *Strange Interlude* takes him inward and downward toward himself, and the plays become increasingly autobiographical. The limits narrow; the subject becomes what lies within himself. The artistic aim is no longer to find God but to know that subject completely. Thus, imagination contracted, and the discipline of *Mourning Becomes Electra* bore unexpected fruit.

There was first paralysis. *Days without End* was a work which he forced to completion, but there is no freedom in it. The work, the last of the theological romances, the final tracing of man's quest for God, is lifeless, contrived; it is knotted, as if in some way the exhaustive work on the trilogy had produced a spasm of the imagination which left O'Neill powerless to continue.

Yet release came. Not for the play he fought to an end, but for another, one in which the imagination found a different outlet and moved easily forward to another country. In September, 1932, while he labored at the third draft of *Days without End*, he awoke remembering the dream of a play. In a long days' work, he wrote out the scenario of *Ah, Wilderness!*, and within six weeks had completed the play. "Only once before," O'Neill said, "has a plot idea [that of *Desire under the Elms*] come to me so easily. I wrote it more easily than I have written any other of my works. . . ." In the midst of the contorted, jammed creative work on *Days without End*, the easy letting-go seemed almost miraculous, a matter for wonder that the imagination could slip its chain and work so spontaneously. The play, however, was the first fruit of the self-discipline of *Mourning Becomes Electra*, and, while the ease was deceptive, the result was prophetic.

Ah, Wilderness! was not entirely the result of a sudden thawing of the imagination. In June, 1931, approximately a month after he and Carlotta O'Neill had returned from their long European exile, the two returned for a day to New London. O'Neill at first looked in vain for his former home, "Monte Cristo Cottage." When he found it, small and unimpressive, surrounded by new construction, he felt it a pitiful thing as the sources of memory revisited often seem. Mrs. O'Neill called the house "a quaint little birdcage," and quoted O'Neill as saying in some dismay that he should not have come. What the sight stirred in him has no easy name. Regret and pain, to be sure, and perhaps more—a sense of debts unpaid and benefits forgot. His life, which in its exterior dimension had gone through a long succession of houses, each more stately than the last, was an encompassing circle around that house, the fixed foot of his movement through the world. Mrs. O'Neill rightly called it a cage, for it was so to O'Neill's spirit. There his needs had formed, his life-in-art begun. The physical return, after a long pilgrimage around the world, is symbolic of a more profound return to his source in anguish of the mind and spirit. He did not enter physically, but the house contained his truth, and he walked it in imagination almost—as the easy genesis of *Ah, Wilderness!* suggests—in spite of himself. Yet not quite. That summer, across the sound from New London, he sketched notes for a play he thought might be titled *Nostalgia*. Later, he wrote to Langner that *Ah, Wilderness!* represented "the paying of an old debt on my part—a gesture toward more comprehensive, unembittered understanding and inner freedom—the breaking away from an old formula I have enslaved myself with." The old, dead world gave on a new creative life.

The sitting room of Nat Miller's house and the living room of the home of James Tyrone in *Long Day's Journey into Night* are in their plan substantially the same, as is the geography of the unseen house beyond it. There are two sets of double doors at the rear, those on the right opening onto a well-lighted front parlor and the stairs to the upper part of the house, those at the left opening onto a dark back parlor, through which access is gained to the dining room and kitchen. An "inoffensive" rug covers both floors, and, although the number and kind of chairs, windows and books differ slightly, the only specific indication of difference is that the wallpaper of the Miller's house is "cheerful," a quality absent from the Tyrone household.

In creating the Miller sitting-room, O'Neill made his first direct incursion on the autobiographical substructure of his life. He entered with joy, colored by nostalgia. With evident delight, he drew in detail the substance of his boyhood world—of the year 1906, when he, like his protagonist, Richard Miller, was seventeen and planning to go to a university in the fall. He created from the citizens he had known in New London, a series of pleasant portraits. The family of the postmaster John McGinley was large, a girl and seven boys, including an Arthur, a Tom, a Lawrence and a Winthrop. The Millers have one girl and five boys, including in addition to Richard an Arthur, a Tommy and two who do not appear, Lawrence and Wilbur. Arthur's close friend is named "Wint." Nat Miller, the editor of the local paper, is based on Fred Latimer, for whom O'Neill worked on the New London *Telegraph*. With no hint of the criticism he had made of her in *Bread and Butter*, he recalled his love affair with Maibelle Scott through Richard's romance with Muriel McComber, and in many other major and minor ways, he portrayed the New London citizenry.

It is the Fourth of July. The town in the grip of an American folk ritual comes vividly to life: fireworks, lodge picnics, outings in the motor car, moonlit beaches, old songs, gardens and, underlying the pleasant manifestations something of the actual economic and social structure of the "large small-town in Connecticut." Within the family, too, O'Neill has used actuality—as, for example, the blue fish "allergy" and the tale of the heroic swimming rescue which Nat Miller tells, and which were both drawn from the repertory of James O'Neill. Like *Mourning Becomes Electra*, the comedy is fixed in a historical perspective, and its evocation of the reality of the past is full and accurate.

That the comedy is also true is a point to be considered. Reading it with the hindsight provided by *Long Day's Journey into Night*, it seems a romantic falsehood, but 1906 was not 1912, the year in which the tragedy was set. By 1912, the books in the sitting-room cases had changed from "boys and girls books and best-selling novels of many past years" to a sterner collection including Nietzsche, Schopenhauer, Marx, Ibsen, Shaw, Strindberg, Swinburne, Rossetti, Wilde, Dowson. As Richard Miller matured to Edmund Tyrone, the books the boy hid on the shelf in his wardrobe were moved downstairs—a small sign of a darkening world closing around the family. O'Neill called the comedy "a dream walking," "a nostalgia for a youth I never had," and spoke of the play's having depicted "the way I would have *liked* my boyhood to have been." At seventeen, however, O'Neill had yet to enter on his renegade and roving life, and there were moments when the sun shone and when laughter was heard in the dark rooms. Reviewers of the original production were reminded of Booth Tarkington's burlesques, of the pangs of adolescence, and pulled forth all the synonyms for "sentimental." At the same time they began to play an autobiographical game, reading "O'Neill" for "Richard Miller." Many of them suggested that at the heart of the matter there lay more than nostalgically glossed reminiscence.

O'Neill's life in 1906, as his biographers have depicted it, was not unhappy. He had learned of his mother's dope addiction when he was fifteen, but in the spring of 1906, she had returned from a sanatorium in good spirits, and gave signs that she might yet overcome her addiction. She had also successfully passed through an operation for a breast tumor. James and she had gone abroad, and in New London, the two O'Neill boys were on their own. Richard Miller, evidently, is more innocent than Eugene was in that year. With Jamie, he made the rounds of bars and occasional brothels, living the life of a young rake with considerable enthusiasm. It was not, however, a dark world he experienced that summer. If he ever had it, the summer of 1906 was a time of freedom from pressure and pain.

Something of this is reflected in *Ah, Wilderness!* The experiences which he assembled to embody the story of a boy "in peg-top trousers [going] the pace that kills along the road to ruin" are fragments of good times—a "dream walking," and like a dream shaping things that were into a thing that never was.

The play has a dream's truth, for under its surface a structure exists that is not easily seen in the play alone. The work contains many ironic echoes of past concerns. As Richard draws Muriel from the shadow into the moonlight on the beach, the movement of light and shadow on the pier when Dion seduces Margaret can be recalled. The poet's sensitiveness, characterized as "a restless, apprehensive, defiant, shy, dreamy, self-conscious intelligence," that marks Richard as O'Neill's fictive self recalls many an earlier hero. So too, Richard, seeking a whore as a defiant gesture against the life he leads, may recall Eben and Dion and Michael Cape. The play's use of sound—the firecrackers, the sound of dance music in the distance, the sense of the turn of the seasons in an unending cycle of life, the use of chiaroscuro, defined by moonlight, are all spun from O'Neill's earlier technique and themes. The difference is that here all events, all "effects" project a sense of well-being and peace, and are not used to go aggressively, painfully "behind life." Yet behind the façade of well-being, as in the substructure of a dream, the truth exists.

However masked, *Ah, Wilderness!* is direct autobiography. In its fictions, he has combined what he has seen and admired outside his life into a disguised version of his own realities. The room, not fog-bound but lighted to brightness by July sun and the moon, is the first clue. The family in the room is the second. Richard's father is wise, able, solicitous, friendly. In all respects, he is responsible and humanly successful. In the house, however, there is another man, Miller's brother-in-law, Sid Davis, merry, but shiftless, a habitué of the Sachem Club and the masculine world of the town. Sid is a failure, as lacking in responsibility as he is in malice. With the wisdom born of drunken experience, he cares for Richard when the boy comes staggering home from his first excursion to the town saloon, standing in loco parentis to the sick child. If Richard's two fathers be combined into one man there would be created the image of a man of talent and potential destroyed by a fatal lack of responsibility. In such a man, failure would emerge as a warping sense of guilt. Superimposed, the two characters suggest a figure not unlike that of O'Neill's father as he drew him in *Long Day's Journey into Night*. Divided, real guilt is dispersed.

Ella O'Neill, depicted as Mary Tyrone in the latter play, showed herself to have qualities of charm. She was, in the early part of the play, solicitous and capable of laughter and love. To the Tyrone men, she is what a mother should be. As the night moves on, these motherly characteristics dislimn, and she turns from her family, withdraws into herself, denies her womanliness and vanishes into the memory of her girlhood before sexual responsibility and its demanding devotions were forced on her. In the Miller household, as with the men, two women are in residence, Richard's mother, in all respects what a mother should be, and her sister-in-law, Lily Miller, a spinster, in love with Sid, yet refusing to accept him as he is and thus denying life by refusing responsibility for love. Their resemblance to Mary is not exact, for neither woman in the comedy is so tortured as the tragic heroine. Yet something of Mary's complex qualities are divided between the two.

The division makes it possible to treat both Sid and Lily gently because responsibility is removed from them as it could not be removed from Ella and James O'Neill. O'Neill, eliminating the crucially identifying details of his father's talent and his mother's addiction, creates the father's sister and the mother's brother. Their frustrated love for one another parallels and silently comments on the love of Nat Miller and his wife, and brings qualities to the whole that move it nearer to the truth without ruining the comedy. From the days of *Beyond the Horizon*, O'Neill had repeatedly brought forth upon his stage characters who stood in closely related opposition to one another: hero and alter ego, man and his double.

The comic tones hide the fact that he has done the same in this play, but it is important to recall that in the fifth draft of *Days without End*, written shortly after *Ah, Wilderness!*, he split the central character into two roles. The division of his father and mother into two roles in *Ah, Wilderness!* alone makes possible their presentation in a comic context.

The freeing of the family members from guilt and responsibility continues. It is not Richard's older brother who introduced Richard to a life of "sin," but the brother's college friend who, ignorant of Richard's virginity, cannot be blamed for leading him astray. Thus Jamie's "stand-in" bears none of Jamie's responsibility for corrupting his younger brother. Significantly too, the family is filled out with another brother, Tommy, and the void left by the death of James O'Neill's second son is filmed over. Richard's own innocence obscures and mitigates Eugene's experience. Eugene, in 1906, has the experience to which Richard pretends. The difference was vast. Richard's introduction to sex is an adolescent fantasy: the "swift baby" from New Haven whom he meets in the night on the town and who tries in vain to coax him to take her upstairs bears no resemblance to the creature who initiated O'Neill into sexual life. In the words of *The Iceman Cometh*, she is a "tart," not a "whore," and sex becomes a naïve posture of the will, not an ugly fact of experience.

The dark currents moving in the play are not to be suspected from the placid surface. The comedy denies them by perfecting imperfections and making pain impossible. Although Richard attempts to move out of the right current of his life, to perform a vindictive, self-destroying act of will, he by no means goes so far as Eugene was to go when he left New London for the bottom of the world. Richard's small excursion passes, and nothing essential is changed. He returns to life, and turns back into the slow cycling seasons. "There he is," his father says as Richard moves into the benevolent, gentle moonlight, which weaves a spell like that of the Caribbean moon: "There he is—like a statue of Love's Young Dream." To his wife Nat quotes *The Rubáiyát*:

> "Yet Ah, that Spring should vanish with the Rose!
> That Youth's sweet-scented manuscript should close!"

And he adds, "Well, Spring isn't everything, is it, Essie? There's a lot to be said for Autumn. That's got beauty, too. And Winter—if you're together." Listeners can barely discern in the closing phrases Cybel's more urgent message to Dion, "Life is all right if you let it alone."

THOMAS F. VAN LAAN

Singing in the Wilderness:
The Dark Vision
of O'Neill's Only Mature Comedy

The consensus about Eugene O'Neill's *Ah, Wilderness!* characterizes the play as nostalgic, light-hearted, sunny, wholly approving of the life and people it depicts, and—in the words of Joseph Wood Krutch—"quite unlike anything else O'Neill ever wrote." O'Neill himself described the play, shortly after he wrote it, as "out of my previous line," and he probably encouraged the usual view by calling it "a comedy of recollection" and "a dream walking," by offering a remarkably noncommittal note for the Wilderness Edition of his plays in which he *seems* to praise "the spirit of the American large small-town at the turn of the century," and by claiming that the play was not autobiographical but "a sort of wishing out loud. That's the way I would have *liked* my boyhood to have been." Since the appearance of *Long Day's Journey into Night*, the consensus has included a realization that *Ah, Wilderness!* dramatizes some of the same material from which O'Neill would eventually create profound tragedy; this realization has generally altered not the response to *Ah, Wilderness!* but merely the terminology in which this response is phrased, for it is now customary to describe the play as the other side of the coin, the "bright counterpart to the dramatist's final self-assessment."

There have, of course, been some departures from this consensus. A few readers—Sheaffer in part, Raleigh in part, Shawcross, and most notably Adler and Carpenter—attribute dark undertones to the play, including a genuine awareness of evil and a suggestion of spiritual despair. However, none of these readers had discussed these undertones in much detail or

From *Modern Drama* 22, no. 1 (March 1979). © 1978 by the University of Toronto, Graduate Centre for the Study of Drama.

sufficiently indicated their sources within the play. Two critics, finally, recoil from *Ah, Wilderness!* with something approaching, and in one case definitely crossing into, loathing. Engel dismisses the play as a falsification of experience, which, among other distortions, bestows upon its heroes, father and son, a set of rewards that "exist only in the sentimental pipe dream." For Ruby Cohn, "*Ah, Wilderness!* conceals smug acceptance of a double standard, hypocrisy of American family life, and unfocused boredom of July 4th, America's national holiday." "Were O'Neill not the author of *Ah, Wilderness!*," Cohn concludes, "it would have faded into the oblivion it deserves."

In one sense, the play *has* virtually faded into oblivion. Many have written about it, but almost no one has attempted to discuss it in detail, to discern exactly what is happening in it and what O'Neill is doing with his supposedly sunny and sentimental material. It is not oblivion that *Ah, Wilderness!* deserves but serious consideration which views it as worthy of the kind of careful, detailed analysis to which O'Neill's other major plays have been subjected and on which all good drama thrives. Analysis of this sort reveals that *Ah, Wilderness!* is far more complex than has yet been realized, that the consensus about the play contains much more sentimentality than the play itself, that the critics who discern dark undertones have apparently merely scratched the surface, and that the sentimentality and smugness of which Engel and Cohn complain stem less from the dramatist than from his characters.

The title of the play, as is well known, constitutes O'Neill's slight modification (changing "Oh" to "Ah") of the first two words in the last line of the most famous quatrain from FitzGerald's translation of *The Rubáiyát of Omar Khayyám*. This quatrain posits a distinction between an existing reality, the wilderness, which is barren, desolate, and lifeless, and the hypothetical transformation of it, "paradise enow," which *could* take place given certain desiderata—the loaf of bread, the jug of wine, and the "thou" singing "beside me." Although most commentators on O'Neill's play treat it as if it dramatized—or sought to—the implicit "paradise enow" evoked by its title, this title in fact emphasizes the wilderness. Perhaps these commentators are in part misled by the "Ah," but as *Webster's New Collegiate Dictionary* explains, "Ah," is an interjection "used to express delight, relief, regret, or contempt," and it would be quite arbitrary to single out any of these usages before seeing which of them the play itself endorses. My reading of the play convinces me that the "ah" of delight belongs chiefly to the characters, who unconsciously or otherwise misperceive the nature of their reality, while their creator, in addition to sharing his characters' misperception to a small degree, is primarily torn between regret and contempt. Far from depicting a paradise—pure or flawed, fool's or otherwise—the play actually depicts a wilderness. The surface light-heartedness, sunniness, and sense of satisfaction are for the most part merely examples of singing in the wilderness—which is a rough equivalent to whistling past a cemetery—by characters who are no more able to face the desolate reality confronting them than are the denizens of Harry Hope's saloon or the four haunted Tyrones.

The fundamental strategy of the play involves something comparable to altering the "ah" of delight to one more suggestive of contempt. *Ah, Wilderness!* emphasizes three familiar American clichés, compares them to the actuality they distort, and concludes that as truths they are sham but as sustaining pipe dreams they are serviceable and necessary. These three clichés, which I list in the order I plan to discuss them, are: first, the gallery of sentimental stereotypes in the mode of Norman Rockwell; second, the Fourth-of-July myth of independence and equality; and third, the notion of family life as the ideal form of existence.

Many readers of *Ah, Wilderness!* have noticed, some of them com-plainingly, the characters' resemblance to key sentimental stereotypes read-ily found in the wish-fulfillment fantasies of the American middle class. Indeed, the opening sequence of the play looks as if O'Neill aimed at nothing other than providing us with whatever satisfactions this resem-blance may afford. This sequence methodically introduces the various members of the family, each of whom is assigned the appropriate appear-ance, manner, language, preoccupations, and activities of a familiar stereo-type. Eleven-year-old Tommy is a cute little dickens, an oh-that-boy! with "a rim of milk visible about his lips." Fifteen-year-old Mildred is the boy-crazy, awkward adolescent girl, largely caught up in teasing her older brothers, especially nineteen-year-old Arthur, who "solemnly collegiate" and self-consciously watchful against assaults upon his dignity, strives manfully but without entire success to appear mature and sophisticated. Mrs. Miller (her name is "Essie," but speech headings and stage directions invariably refer to her as "Mrs. Miller") possesses "a bustling mother-of-a-family manner"; she is "the Mother's Day Mother," as Engel calls her, pointedly deferential to her husband, constantly hovering over her brood to correct and protect. Aunt Lily, shy and kindly, "conforms outwardly to the conventional type of old-maid school teacher, even to wearing glasses." Mrs. Miller's brother, Sid Davis, "with the puckish face of a Peck's Bad Boy who has never grown up," is the carefree, jovial, fun-loving uncle. Nat Miller is the "understanding and ever-smiling father," who, as befits the head of the household, governs his various charges with a fine balance of severity and indulgence.

What has not been clearly realized about these stereotypes is that O'Neill by no means intends that we perceive them as the actual identities of his characters; on the contrary, he soon defines them—for the adult members of the family, at least—as roles that his characters have adopted or have had imposed on them. The idea of behavior as role-playing is familiar enough in O'Neill's plays, and it is explicitly established in *Ah, Wilderness!* by the clownish antics of Sid and the tortured posing of Richard Miller, who is a prototype for Con Melody of *A Touch of the Poet*. Richard, moreover, is called a "child actor," and both he and Sid, we hear at separate times, "ought to be on the stage." But even before Richard enters and Sid fully warms up, the idea of role-playing has already been implicitly introduced through the difficulty Lily and Sid have in trying to maintain the stereotypes associated with them. Sid would genuinely like to be the jovial uncle, but his drinking and Lily's attitude toward it fill him with self-loathing and self-pity, and so he is driven to melodramatic overacting in his vain efforts to turn his situation into a joke. Lily pretends to find contentment in her husbandless and childless lot, but she cannot—or will not—conceal her underlying anguish and particularly the pain that Sid's weakness constantly causes her. The discrepancy between Lily's mask and her reality is most fully revealed in act 2, and it is at this same time that Mrs. Miller, with the men gone, drops her normal pose as the deferential, reverent wife. "Men are weak," she assures Lily, and a few minutes later, as she talks about tricking Nat into eating bluefish, she reveals how she actually feels about his opinions; and since she believes that she not only can but ought to deceive him, she also reveals her convictions of her own superiority.

The ubiquitous discrepancy between pose and actuality is perhaps most interesting and most important in the case of Nat Miller, however, because readers of the play almost uniformly see him as the embodiment of an ideal type. O'Neill may use greater subtlety with Nat than with the others, but he nonetheless manages, and in several ways, to indicate that for Nat, too, the surface is a mask that cannot quite conceal the reality lurking behind it. I shall here point to only one instance. During his confrontation with McComber, Nat loses his temper, thereby momentarily forfeiting his role as all-wise controller of every situation. But this fact is of less significance than what it occasions after McComber leaves, for here Nat must assure Sid (and evidently himself) that his loss of control is not characteristic of him, and he must elicit from Sid reassurances that he really is what everyone who knows him regards him to be. It is clear from this episode that while Nat is not always able to be what he wants to be—or thinks he has to be—he is also determined that no one, including himself, will be permitted fully to discern his failure.

It is Richard who alerts us to the second cliché examined in *Ah, Wilderness!*, the Fourth-of-July myth of independence and equality, when shortly after his initial entrance, he bursts out in vehement denunciation: "I don't believe in this silly celebrating the Fourth of July—all this lying talk about liberty—when there is no liberty . . . ! The land of the free and the home of the brave! Home of the slave is what they ought to call it—the wage slave ground under the heel of the capitalist class, starving, crying for bread for his children, and all he gets is a stone! The Fourth of July is a stupid farce!" Richard's denunciations remind us that the era in which the Millers lived also knew social injustice and human suffering of a sort that none of the Millers or their friends had ever experienced and that all of them, Richard included, are ignorant of or indifferent to. But Richard's excessive, adolescent rhetoric and the responses of his father (a twinkle in the eye, a scarcely concealed grin) define the speaker of these denunciations as a buffoon, and this definition allows us either to dismiss the denunciations as irrelevant, or, worse yet, to laugh off or laugh at the abuses and suffering they invoke. On the other hand, O'Neill undoubtedly expected some members of his audience to experience a more complicated relation to this material, and to be troubled not only by the callowness of Richard's version of these issues and Nat's complacent indifference to them but also by the ease with which they themselves have been provoked to laughter about matters deserving a response of a much different kind.

More important than the immediate impact of Richard's denunciations—whatever it may be—is the fact that the contrast he introduces here pertains even to the narrow world that the play directly depicts. The immediate milieu of *Ah, Wilderness!* is innocent of sweatshops and starving children, but even the Millers and their associates exist within an oppressive social reality that diverges sharply from the independence and equality promised by the myth. This social reality is what causes the characters of the play to engage in their role-playing, the reason for which is twofold. On the one hand, they are trying to conform to an established network of roles which they assume to be valid. On the other, this network is so oppressive for most if not all of them that they try to lose themselves in its individual units in the same way that other O'Neill characters turn to sustaining pipe dreams. They try to convince themselves that they *are* what they have to be in order to ward off the pain and anguish caused by their having to be exactly that.

What makes this network of roles oppressive is the fact that it has been cast in the form of a rigid hierarchy that relegates most of its members to outcast or second-class status. The clearest example of an outcast, and hence a representative of the bottom of the hierarchy, is Belle, the prostitute, everybody's victim, whom we last see, appropriately, being brutalized by the Bartender. The Bartender himself is not much better off; he is, after all, striking out at her because of his own vulnerability, expressed in his fear that Nat Miller will have him "run . . . out of town" for serving drinks to his son. The second-class citizens abound, for they include all children, all women, and all males who for some reason fall short: as Arthur does, in part because he is not yet quite a man and in part simply because his father dislikes him; as McComber does, because he lacks a sense of proper proportions; and as Sid does, because he is totally without self-discipline. Perched on top of this hierarchy—albeit, as we have seen, a bit precariously—is Nat Miller, who holds this position because he is a respectable, professionally successful, adult male with more common sense, wisdom, and self-discipline than the other adult males of the play.

In relation to Nat, according to the language of the play, the other characters lack full adult status. McComber has sufficient age, but he is an "old fool" and an "old idiot". Arthur, though nineteen, is at one point ordered by his father to "skedaddle" with the rest of the "kids." Belle and her kind, according to Sid, are "babies," while Sid himself, according to Richard on one occasion, is "a bigger kid than Tommy is." Interestingly enough—since O'Neill is not only demonstrating the existence of the hierarchy but also implicitly criticizing it—as Nat Miller heads for bed at the end of the play, he asks his wife's permission to skip his prayers; "You're worse than Tommy!" she exclaims fondly, but then with a note of motherly indulgence she grants his request.

O'Neill dramatizes this hierarchy throughout the play and by a variety of means, including the entire scene in the bar, Nat's belittling generalizations about women, the joke which assumes that women and children are unfit to know the specific "wickedness" committed by Oscar Wilde, and Nat's refusal to take Richard's rebellious protests more seriously than as signs of a stage he is passing through. To my mind, however, the episode that most strikingly evokes the hierarchy and its implications is the one in which Nat sends his wife out of the room in order to have a man-to-man talk with Richard. Readers of the play who mention this scene praise it for its humor and for the fine impression of Nat and of the father-son relationship that it conveys. The scene has funny moments certainly, but as often in *Ah, Wilderness!*, the humor is subtly blended with nasty undertones that threaten to turn humor into satire. For what Nat accomplishes, in effect, is to enlighten Richard with regard to one of the ways in which "human society [is] organized": the fact that "a certain class of women" has been set aside for the purpose of satisfying the sexual needs of the male members of society. Nat concedes that it is probably best to avoid "girls like that" entirely, but, after all, human nature *is* human nature, and the only real wrong, from his point of view, would be "to ever get mixed up with them seriously": "You just have what you want and pay 'em and forget it."

If the third cliché examined in *Ah, Wilderness!*, the idealization of family life, were true, then most of its characters would remain unaffected by the oppressive social reality encompassing them, because they participate in family life and thus have constant access to the loving nurturance it supposedly provides. In some ways the play seems to be an endorsement of the notion that middle-class family life is the ideal form of existence, especially when Richard and Muriel vow to marry someday, and when, at the end of the play, Nat and Mrs. Miller affirm that being together lends beauty to the autumn and even to the winter—that, in other words, it is an effective means for converting wilderness to paradise. One must not, however, emphasize these final notes at the expense of countless earlier notes insisting that, far from compensating for the wilderness of existence, family life in fact constitutes one of its most oppressive elements. These notes, located throughout the play, occur in special abundance in two of its scenes, act three, scene two, in which the other members of the family await Richard's late-night return, and the dinner scene that takes up the second half of act two.

The latter episode is among the best scenes O'Neill wrote. It is extremely funny and yet, at the same time, it makes us painfully aware of how harrowing domestic existence can be. According to this scene, the function of the family is not to nurture and sustain but to curb and inhibit, and, alternatively, to provide captive victims for relieving one's hurt and frustration. If one member of the family expresses exuberance, as Nat does when he "slaps [his wife] jovially on her fat buttocks," this necessarily causes distress or worse to another, and the victim must immediately find relief by turning to attack some member of the family who is in an even more vulnerable position. If one member of the family tries to assert his individuality by indulging some idiosyncrasy—as Nat does in imagining bluefish poisons him or in endlessly retelling the same stories about himself—he cannot simply be ignored or tolerated; he must instead be made a laughing-stock so that he will learn to conform—though it is far more likely that he will instead precipitate an attack on one of the others, most probably the one who was least involved in the attack on him. There is by no means any vast gulf between the family dynamics of this episode and the far more obviously destructive interaction uniting the Tyrones of *Long Day's Journey into Night*. Interestingly enough, moreover, both plays include a servant girl who suggests a better way. In act three of *Long Day's Journey*, as Mary Tyrone complains to Cathleen about her husband's many failings, thereby assigning blame for her torment and suffering, she is unable to shake the servant girl's dogged conviction that Tyrone—and, it is implied, all people—is to be accepted, no matter what his faults. And Cathleen is merely echoing the Millers' Norah, who cheerfully excuses Sid's outrageous behavior at dinner with "Ah, Miss Lily, don't mind him. He's only under the influence. Sure, there's no harm in him at all."

It might be objected to this reading of *Ah, Wilderness!* that O'Neill does, after all, end his play with the emphatic notes of affirmation already referred to. In response, four points can be made. First, and this is a possibility offered without much insistence, no dramatist wants to alienate totally the potential audience upon whom the commercial success of his work depends. Second, although the vision of the Millers' world which O'Neill presents is a dark one, *in form* he never entirely breaks with the genre of nostalgic family comedy, and this ending is appropriate to the genre. Third, it should be noted that these final scenes of affirmation are drenched in moonshine, and this is perhaps O'Neill's way of suggesting that his characters are here behaving pretty much as they do in act three, scene two, when Arthur sings his sentimental songs and the other Millers instantly surrender to the maudlin lure. Additional suspicious qualities of the very last episode include Nat's acting like a big kid (in trying to get out of his prayers), the suggestions that the characters are striking poses rather than behaving spontaneously (Nat's "Let her go, Gallagher" and his perceiving Richard as "like a statue of Love's Young Dream,"), and the final stage direction, which has Nat and Mrs. Miller moving "back into the darkness of the front parlor."

The fourth point, which seems to me to afford the interpretation most responsive to the play, can perhaps best be approached through considering O'Neill's presentation of his central character, Richard Miller. Richard is caught between two locations of the hierarchy, the child who he has been and to whom he frequently returns, and the man who he is supposed to become. His rebellious outbursts and actions are the result of his efforts to play the man in the only way he can conceive of, since he is as yet unable to fulfill the requirements for doing so in the approved manner, that of his father. By the end of the play, however, it is clear that he is well on his way toward fulfilling these requirements, and his father can affirm with relief, "I don't think we'll ever have to worry about his being safe—from himself—again." Richard's reading, as is well known, reflects that of his creator; so also does the content of his outbursts; and Richard is the only character in the play who is at all in touch with the critical attitude O'Neill has toward the smug complacency of the Millers' narrow world. Yet O'Neill, as well as Nat, sees Richard in his rebellious attitudinizing as a figure more of mirth than of truth, and he presents Richard's development in the later scenes not as the tragic loss of a possibility for full emancipation but, in Bogard's terms, as a reclamation, as a return to the proper path.

To some extent this presentation of Richard can be accounted for as a response to genre—comedy often views any deviation from the social norm as preposterous, and nostalgic family comedy demands an harmonious conclusion. But there is also present here, it seems to me, a genuine ambivalence on O'Neill's part which is typical of his entire relationship to the material of *Ah, Wilderness!*. Despite his critical attitude, O'Neill never wholly succeeds in detaching himself—or us—from the values in which the Millers try to believe. In the same way that he is able to laugh at Richard, and make us laugh at him, even while no doubt privately agreeing with what Richard has to say, he also, I think, genuinely tries to find something worth celebrating in the Millers' existence and to celebrate it. However, he is too knowledgeable about the human capacity for self-deception, and too honest in reporting accurately what he sees, to submit with any deep conviction to the sentimental pipe dream most of the characters have accepted. As a result, *Ah, Wilderness!* is a much richer and more interesting play than it is generally taken to be.

JEAN CHOTHIA

Long Day's Journey into Night:
The Dramatic Effectiveness of Supposedly Neutral Dialogue

In *Long Day's Journey into Night*, there are four major characters. Whatever variety or intensity, sadness or humor the play has must come from the dialogue and gesture of these four. When he creates a stage presence for his characters, O'Neill is conscious of the effect of their speech and of their physical being. In the stage directions, he notes not only costume and appearance, but bearing and quality of voice. Tyrone

> is sixty-five but looks ten years younger . . . his bearing . . . has
> a soldierly quality of head up, chest out, stomach in, shoulders
> squared . . . a big, finely shaped head . . . His voice is remarka-
> bly fine, resonant and flexible . . . There is a lot of solid earthy
> peasant in him.

and the description is complemented by a speech mode that is equally robust and straightforward.

The majority of Tyrone's sentences fall into the subject—verb—complement pattern of the normal English sentence. The subject is usually a personal pronoun and only rarely a nominal phrase or clause. The sentences are usually simple or coordinating and there are few adjuncts. When O'Neill wants to intensify Tyrone's speech he does so by adding one or two new elements or by concentrating the habitual syntax and making it strikingly regular. In act 4, for example, when Tyrone in one of the crucial

From *Forging a Language: A Study of the Plays of Eugene O'Neill.* © 1979 by Cambridge University Press.

speeches of the play confesses to Edmund that he has betrayed his dreams
for financial security, his self-searching is conveyed by just such grammati-
cal intensification:

> I've never admitted this to anyone before . . . *That God-damned*
> *play* I bought for a song and made such a great success in—a
> great money success—*it* ruined me with its promise of an easy
> fortune. I didn't want to do anything else, and by the time I
> woke up to the fact I'd become a slave to the damned thing
> and did try other plays it was too late. They had identified me
> with that one part, and didn't want me in anything else. They
> were right, too. I'd lost the great talent I once had through
> years of easy repetition, never learning a new part, never really
> working hard. Thirty-five to forty thousand dollars net profit a
> season like snapping your fingers! It was too great a tempta-
> tion. Yet before I bought the damned thing I was considered
> one of the three or four young actors with the greatest artistic
> promise in America. I'd worked like hell. I'd left a good job as
> a machinist to take supers' parts because I loved the theatre. I
> was wild with ambition. I read all the plays ever written. I
> studied Shakespeare as you'd study the Bible. I educated myself.
> I got rid of an Irish Brogue you could cut with a knife. I loved
> Shakespeare. I would have acted in any of his plays for nothing,
> for the joy of being alive in his great poetry. And I acted well in
> him. I felt inspired by him. I could have been a great Shake-
> spearian actor if I'd kept on. I know that! [my italics]

The confession begins with a more complicated construction than is usual
in Tyrone's speech. The subject is not a simple noun ("The play") but is a
nominal group ("That God-damned play") which contains besides adjectives and nouns, two post modifying clauses ("[which] I bought" and
"[which I] made such a." It is disjoined from its verb and placed in
apposition to the pronoun, "it". Randolph Quirk has noted that this type
of construction is common in spoken English where it is used for emphasis
and clarity and, certainly, the unusually complicated syntax here, does
suggest Tyrone's anxiety to communicate a difficult insight into himself as
accurately as possible. The impression is reinforced by Tyrone's use of
parenthetical intensifiers, "They were right, too"; "I know that", and,
later in the speech, "And it was true"; "Ask her what I was like in those
days." Tyrone's speech seems to become more animated when he recalls

the crucial period in his past. His normally preferred construction becomes completely dominant, "I read . . . I studied . . . I educated . . . I got rid of . . . I loved," and the succession of short parallel sentences makes the distant experience seem close, until the simple past tense gives way to the hypothetical past tense in two conditional clauses, "I *would* have acted . . . for nothing . . . I *could* have been . . . a great Shakespearean actor," reminding us that all the effort and devotion was forfeit and pushing the events back into the distant past.

Syntax is similarly important in structuring our response to the words of the other characters. O'Neill seems to take us into Jamie's mind in the course of his confession in act 4. After a sequence of boisterous camaraderie, Jamie introduces a more serious note into the conversation:

> Nix, Kid! You listen! Did it on purpose to make a bum of you. Or part of me did. A big part. That part that's been dead so long. That hates life. My putting you wise so you'd learn from my mistakes. Believed that myself at times, but it's a fake. *Made* my mistakes look good. *Made* getting drunk romantic. *Made* whores fascinating vampires instead of poor, stupid, diseased slobs they really are. *Made* fun of work as a sucker's game. Never wanted you succeed and make me look even worse by comparison. Wanted you to fail. Always jealous of you. Mama's baby, Papa's pet! (*He stares at Edmund with increasing enmity.*) And it was your being born that started Mama on dope. I know that's not your fault, but all the same, God damn you, I can't help hating your guts—! [my italics]

The parataxis at the beginning has much the same function as the complicated syntax at the opening of Tyrone's speech. Jamie is reaching around for his meaning. Then, in a succession of parallel sentences beginning "Made," we are presented with a catalogue of Jamie's self-blame until, at the end of the passage, the self-blame is suddenly replaced by accusation. The shift in thought is marked by the significantly childish insult, "Mama's baby, Papa's pet!," after which we have the impression of a deeper, darker impulse overcoming the original goodwill of the confession. A syntactical shift underlines the change, signalling that we have moved to a different level of Jamie's consciousness. He himself says later that he had not meant to tell "that last stuff," adding "Don't know what made me." Obviously, we do not respond to the grammar at a conscious level noting, "Ah, parataxis! Ah, a syntactical shift!," but we can see how instrumental the syntactical shift is if we try to rewrite the passage substituting a continuation of the elliptical pattern of the earlier part of the speech for the complete sentences with which the passage concludes in O'Neill's text. If we read, for example, "Wanted you to fail. Always jealous of you. Resented your being born. Said started Mama on dope. Know not your fault, but can't help hating you," we find that the change from self-blame to self-justification is lost and, with it, the impression the last part of the passage gives of suppressed thoughts spilling over into speech. In both confessions, O'Neill communicates the secret emotion of his characters through his structuring of their speech. The audience is made to feel something about the characters without being conscious of the machinery that shapes their feeling.

Tyrone is given an alternative register of speech, which is used when he is hurt, embarrassed or angry, and acts as a kind of subliminal preparation for his confession. Although he is given particularly resonant quotations from Shakespeare to roll around the theatre with his fine and flexible voice, his alternative register is not the prose of Shakespearean drama but that of the melodramatic stage. In this mode, colourful nominal phrases replace the pronouns—Shaughnessey, for example, is "that blackguard" —and a string of synonymous verbs or a succession of imperatives replace his normal verb pattern. In act 2, for example, Tyrone berates Jamie:

> You ought to be kicked out in the gutter! But if I did it, you
> know damn well who'd weep and plead for you, and excuse
> you and complain till I let you come back.

On such occasions, he adopts not only the speech structure but the attitudes of melodrama. The register is made to appear more flamboyant because it is used most frequently in argument with Jamie, whose speech on such occasions is terse.

O'Neill uses the histrionic side of Tyrone to bring vigour and variety to the play's surface. We enjoy Tyrone's delight in recitation and fine words and relish his flourishing gestures when we see them or hear them described, as for instance by Mary who describes the stage bow she sees him direct towards haughty neighbours passing in their smart car. In act 4, O'Neill produces a brilliant *coup de théâtre*. A squabble between Tyrone and Edmund, developed from a petty clash of wills over whether the lights should be turned off or not, becomes bitter when Edmund taunts his father with his meanness and bigotry. The angry tirade with which Tyrone replies is stilled on his recollecting his son's illness and, in one of those moments of sudden quiet which O'Neill creates from time to time between the members of this family, Edmund, ashamed, gets up to turn out the lights. He is forestalled by his father whose anger is replaced by an equally overstated self-pity, accompanied by a magnificent gesture:

> Let it burn! (*He stands up abruptly—and a bit drunkenly— and begins turning on the three bulbs in the chandelier, with a childish, bitterly dramatic self-pity.*) We'll have them all on! Let them burn! To hell with them! The poorhouse is the end of the road, and it might as well be sooner as later! (*He finishes turning on the lights.*)

The whole quarrel has collapsed into broad comedy.

But O'Neill does not create such a dramatic moment without integrating it into the structure of the play. Drinking and brooding over Mary, occasionally returning to their card game, the two men again become hostile when Edmund accuses his father of planning to send him to a cheap sanatorium in order not to waste money on attempting to cure a fatal disease. The vicious aspect of Tyrone's meanness is felt more sharply because the audience has enjoyed its comic aspect. This cruel exchange exposes a rawer level of emotion and, in order to make the return from this extreme position, O'Neill must present us with something as intense in a positive instead of a negative way. It is here that he introduces Tyrone's confession. When Tyrone concludes with the wry inquiry, "What the hell was it I wanted to buy, I wonder?," his claim on our sympathy has been reestablished. But, suddenly, the initial obstinacy and the splendid gesture are recalled and the audience are shifted back to the humour of the beginning of the sequence, when Tyrone says:

> The glare from those extra lights hurts my eyes. You don't mind
> if I turn them out do you? We don't need them, and there's no
> use making the Electric Company rich.

The conflict between our recognition of Tyrone's uncertainty and broken dream and our sense of the ridiculous ensures that our response to James Tyrone will remain ambivalent. If we recall the melodramatic stage clichés which swamped O'Neill's writing at the beginning of his career when he attempted to convey strong emotion [discussed elsewhere] and compare the strategic use to which they are put here, we have some measure of the kind of control O'Neill is exerting.

O'Neill uses contrast between the melodramatic and the plain-speaking register, to create an impression of heartfelt sincerity in Tyrone in sentences which, out of context, would seem neutral enough. He sometimes does this by a direct juxtaposition as in this utterance, for example, when the register of Tyrone's attempt to comfort Edmund in the first part contrasts with that in his apostrophizing of Jamie in the second part:

> don't take it too much to heart, lad. He loves to exaggerate the worst of himself when he's drunk. He's devoted to you. It's the one good thing left in him. (*He looks down on Jamie with a bitter sadness.*) A sweet spectacle for me! My first born, who I hoped would bear my name in honour and dignity, who showed such brilliant promise!

At other times, our recognition of what Mary's surrender to the drug means to the family is sharpened because words fail the usually fluent Tyrone. In act 2, when it is apparent that Mary has yielded to the drug, Tyrone remains slumped and silent. One of the most moving moments of the play comes later when Tyrone simply cries out his wife's name, and then adds a brief appeal, "For the love of God, for my sake and the boys' sake and your own, won't you stop now?" The actor in the theatre uttering the cry, can hardly fail to make use of the long gliding dipthong in the final word, drawing on the very sound of the word to express the pain. Under pressure of strong emotion we may, as Yeats has suggested, be capable only of looking "silently into the fireplace" but, if the appropriate context has been created, those will be speaking silences.

At the beginning of the play, O'Neill emphasizes how normal the manner and matter of Mary Tyrone's speech is. She has the preoccupations and the slang of polite middle class America ("I've gotten too fat, you mean. I really ought to reduce"; "As soon as your head touches the pillow"; "I do feel out of sorts"; "You must have gotten out of the wrong side of the bed this morning"). She is self-possessed, rarely speaking except to pacify. In the first draft of the play, O'Neill made Mary's speech tense and erratic at the outset, but he later cut the explicit signals of her anxiety so that now the implication that she is not as calm as she might appear filters in only slowly and does so primarily through gesture—a hand patting hair, fingers drumming on the table top, and through two quickly curtailed outbursts. A hardly stated impression of resentment is conveyed through a series of comments which, individually, would appear as light teasing of Tyrone but, taken together, form a complaint. The audience are alerted to her unease by the conversation between Jamie and Tyrone during Mary's first absence and, from this point onwards, have a new sensitivity to the implications of her utterance. At her return, Mary replies to Jamie's comment that Hardy is not a good doctor:

> Oh. No, I wouldn't say he was either. (*Changing the subject—forcing a smile.*) That Bridget! I thought I'd never get away. She told me all about her second cousin on the police force in St Louis. (*Then with nervous irritation.*) Well, if you're going to work on the hedge why don't you go? (*Hastily.*) I mean, take advantage of the sunshine before the fog comes back. (*Strangely, as if talking aloud to herself.*) Because I know it will. (*Suddenly she is self-consciously aware that they are both staring fixedly at her—flurriedly, raising her hands.*) Or I should say, the rheumatism in my hands knows. It's a better weather prophet than you are, James. (*She stares at her hands with fascinated repulsion.*) Ugh! How ugly they are! Who'd ever believe they were once beautiful.

In such a speech, O'Neill rewards the expectations he has created and stimulates further concentration. We miss Mary's earlier coherence. The individual sentences are neutral enough, what makes them striking is their erratic combination. She seems to respond to some private significance in her seemingly commonplace remarks which she hastens to qualify. Each sentence begins with a conjunction or a parenthetical phrase, as though she were beginning mid-sentence. The distracted movement of her speech is ominous, following the men's discussion, and so is the harshness with which she rebuffs Jamie's attempt to reassure her at the end of the scene.

Towards the end of the first act, therefore, Mary's probable return to the drug is signalled by the shape of her speech. In the subsequent acts, the fragmentation of her personality under the drug is also imaged in the structure of her speech. In acts 2 and 3, O'Neill presents us with an extraordinary study of the human mind under the influence of morphine. Freed from the normal restraints of intercourse, Mary speaks her fears and harboured resentments, her impulsive warmth and her perceptions about the personality of others. She moves in panic between the present and the past in search of the explanation of her suffering until, in act 4, she comes to rest, cut off from reality, at a point of security in the distant past.

Four main patterns alternate in Mary's speech in acts 2 and 3, and one slowly comes to dominate. One pattern recurs when Mary is obliged to deal with present anxieties. Her speech then becomes frenetic, a combination of excited protests and nagging questions, with which she torments both herself and the men:

> Why is that glass there? Did you take a drink? Oh, how can you be such a fool? Don't you know it's the worst thing? You're to blame, James. How could you let him?

> I won't have it! Do you hear, Edmund? Such morbid nonsense! . . . Your father shouldn't allow you.

> I won't have it! How dare . . . ! How dare . . . ! What right . . . ?

The busy persistence of such speeches and the uniformity of their tone make them hard to listen to and present a distressing contrast with the peacemaking Mary of act 1. O'Neill establishes a guilty allegiance between the audience and the listening characters by following such outbursts with an abrupt and unsympathetic demand for peace from one of the men: "Mama, stop talking!"; "Stop talking crazy," and, more harshly, in protection of a third person, "Mary! Hold your tongue." When Mary finally arrives at her resting place, isolated from the present, the audience's response is qualified by a feeling of relief at being able to listen easily to her words.

There is also a vein of quiet sharpness in Mary's speech. She utters words lightly which are not light for the character who hears them. Nothing is explicitly stated—the onus of making the connection between the two figures present before them on the stage being put on to the audience, who thus become acutely conscious of the emotion of the silent listener. This is not a new device for O'Neill, although it is used more consistently here than elsewhere. In the first part of *Mourning Becomes Electra*, for example, the inert dialogue briefly comes alive in a speech in which Christine says of the Mannon house:

> Each time I come back after being away it appears more like a sepulchre! The "whited" one of the Bible—pagan temple front stuck like a mask on Puritan grey ugliness! It was just like old Abe Mannon to build such a monstrosity—as a temple for his hatred. (*Then with a little mocking laugh.*) Forgive me, Vinnie. I forgot you liked it.

Her mocking apology, alerting us to the significance of the words for her listening daughter, are more telling than all Lavinia's lengthy reminiscences of her mother's failure to love her as a child. Mary's words can seem as cutting, as they do, for example, in the sequence which comes after Mary has recalled her first meeting with Tyrone. He replies to her query, "Do you remember?":

> TYRONE (*deeply moved—his voice husky*). Can you think I'd ever forget, Mary? (*Edmund looks away from them sad and embarrassed.*)
>
> MARY (*tenderly*). No. I know you still love me, James, in spite of everything.
>
> TYRONE (*His face works and he blinks back tears—with quiet intensity.*) Yes! As God is my judge! Always and forever, Mary!
>
> MARY. And I love you, dear, in spite of everything.
> (*There is a pause in which Edmund moves embarrassedly. The strange detachment comes over her manner again as if she were speaking impersonally of people seen from a distance.*)
> But I must confess, James, although I couldn't help loving you, I would never have married you if I'd known you drank so much.

The calmness of the repudiation after the moment of intimacy makes it seem particularly cruel. Later in the same act, O'Neill uses the device over an extended sequence of the action, rousing and then undercutting the audience's feelings of hostility to Mary. Edmund exposes his misery to his mother in a desperate attempt to draw sympathy from her. She rebuffs him with a light denial:

> You're so like your father, dear. You love to make a scene out of nothing so you can be dramatic and tragic. If I gave you the slightest encouragement you'd tell me next you were going to die—

and then, when her son has left in despair, replies with shocking indifference to Tyrone's query about him, "Perhaps he's going uptown again to find Jamie. He still had some money left, I suppose." The contrast between this and her sudden bare cry, "Oh, James, I'm so frightened. I know he's going to die," which is accompanied by her reaching out for physical contact and then sobbing, is distressing, and confuses our certainty of who is strong and who weak, who caring and who cruel. The emotional force of the device depends on the audience's consciousness of the listener and, therefore, belongs peculiarly to the drama where we can watch one character whilst listening to the other. As we shall see, the auditor's consciousness of the tangled emotions of the silent listeners, is used to remarkable effect in the final line of the play.

The audience is made aware of the inconsistencies in Mary's self-portrayal. Her regret at not having become a nun, for example, must be accommodated with Cathleen's astonishment at the notion, with her delight in describing her wedding dress, and with her account of her first meeting with Tyrone, in which the details confront us not with a nun but with a coquettish schoolgirl concerned about the redness of her eyes and nose. Sometimes O'Neill shows us a Mary who veers within a single speech from one line of thought to another, from one emotion to another, contradicting in one sentence the idea of the previous one. This third pattern in her speech gives us the impression of her incoherence without ever being allowed to become itself incoherent because O'Neill limits its use to a few strategic points in the action. It occurs in the utterance which tells Tyrone she has returned to the drug; again, immediately after the three men have left (act 2); immediately before they re-enter (act 3); at the end of her long recollection of the past, when her excursion to buy the drug is discussed, and, finally, when she briefly faces the truth about Edmund's illness. These are all occasions on which the present intrudes on her reverie about the past or she is forced to acknowledge her close ties with one of the three men.

My example is the monologue spoken before the men's entrance in act 3:

> You're a sentimental fool. What is so wonderful about that first meeting between a silly romantic schoolgirl and a matinee idol? You were much happier before you knew he existed, in the Convent when you used to pray to the Blessed Virgin. (*Longingly.*) If I could only find the faith I lost, so I could pray again! (*She pauses—then begins to recite the Hail Mary in a flat, empty tone.*) "Hail, Mary, full of grace! The Lord is with Thee; blessed art Thou among women." (*Sneeringly.*) You expect the Blessed Virgin to be fooled by a lying dope fiend reciting words! You can't hide from Her! (*She springs to her feet. Her*

hands fly up to pat her hair distractedly.) I must go upstairs. I haven't taken enough. When you start again you never know exactly how much you need. (*She goes toward the front parlour—then stops in the doorway as she hears the sound of voices from the front path. She starts guiltily.*) That must be them—(*She hurries back to sit down. Her face sets in stubborn defensiveness—resentfully.*) Why are they coming back? They don't want to. And I'd much rather be alone. (*Suddenly her whole manner changes. She becomes pathetically relieved and eager.*) Oh, I'm so glad they've come! I've been so horribly lonely!

Clearly, the interpretation and voice control of the actress are extremely important in creating the effect of such speeches but the dramatist guides her with his structuring of the passage as well as with his stage directions about tone and bearing. Mary uses the second person pronoun to address herself in her expressions of self-contempt at the opening of her speech. This somewhat impersonal form gives way to the first person pronoun when she speaks longingly and the thrusting questions and accusations are replaced by the conditional form of the verb. The epithets she applies to herself, "sentimental fool," "silly romantic schoolgirl," are bitter enough when contrasted with the joyfulness we heard in her account of that meeting a few speeches earlier but they are, nevertheless, the same kind of language. When, soon afterwards, she calls herself a "lying dope fiend" we have the impression that there has been a real mental shift, because Mary is now using a different and cruder kind of slang. In the last section of the monologue, her contradictory response to the men's return is expressed by the juxtaposition of a snatch of Mary's nagging, questioning, with a snatch of the register which we have heard frequently in the central acts and which will dominate her speech at the end of the play.

We are prepared for the state of withdrawal which Mary will have achieved at the end of the play by her own testimony and by that of the men. "She'll listen but she won't listen. She'll be here but she won't be here," says Jamie, and Tyrone endorses this, "Yes . . . there'll be the same drifting away from us until by the end of each night—." And equally suggestive, if less explicit, are the other comments: "If you're that far gone in the past already, when it's only the afternoon, what will you be tonight?"; "You're not so far gone yet . . . ," and, finally, when it is already late evening, Edmund predicts, "She'll be nothing but a ghost haunting the past by this time . . . Back before I was born—," and Tyrone replies, "Doesn't she do the same with me? Back before she ever knew me." And

the words "far," "back," "beyond," "far away" recur in that part of
Mary's speech, the fourth strand that we find in acts 2 and 3 which I will
call "reverie." As we listen to the various passages of reverie, we realize
that it is not one particular event Mary is trying to retrieve, but a state of
mind: of faith, perhaps, but faith in herself as well as in the Deity, and
faith that there is meaning and purpose in existence. She searches back
into her past until she finds a time when life was forward looking, and
there were still choices to be made.

O'Neill underlines this by using as the language of reverie, the eager,
effusive elements of girlish speech. "Lovely," "beautiful," "dreadful" are
recurrent adjectives. The same word is repeated with a different function
or meaning within a brief section of her utterance: "All" is used like this in
act 3, "I forgot *all* about . . . *All* I wanted was . . . And in *all* those
thirty-six years . . . ," and "sure" in the final speech of the play, "how *sure*
. . . to make me *sure* . . . as *surely* as . . . I must be more *sure* . . . If I was
so *sure* . . . If I still felt *sure*." The impression of trusting naïveté, so
moving when heard from the mouth of the white-haired woman, cruelly
worn by her experience of the world, is conveyed by the use of "and" to
pile up adjectives in descriptions of people and events: of Tyrone, for
instance, who was "simple, and kind, and unassuming, not a bit stuck up
or vain," or of Mother Elizabeth, who is lovingly described in the final
speech. It is conveyed, too, by the use of school-girl slang, "stuck-up,"
"my good points," "all mixed up," and girlish intensifiers, "I was *really*
shocked," "her eyes look *right* into your heart," "it was *simply* a waste of
time," "I was *so* mad at myself." We begin to see here how effectively
O'Neill uses the seemingly insignificant words in presenting a verbal image
of personality. Indeed, the use of the intensifier "so" recurs at crucial
moments of the play and becomes remarkably expressive as a result. "I
worked *so* hard," "I was *so* bashful," "I was *so* excited and happy": such
remarks occur frequently in the reverie and show us Mary at her most
girlish, untouched by disappointment. To express Mary's present desolation,
O'Neill uses the same construction, but combines "so" with "alone,"
"lonesome," or "lonely." The assonance here on the "o" sound is even
more striking in Standard American than in Standard English because the
vowel sound can be held on to longer when uttered with an American
intonation. The echoing cry "so lonely" is fixed more securely in the
auditor's mind because not only are these the last words Mary speaks
before the men enter in act 3, but they have also been uttered as the final
words of act 2, scene 2, the mid-point of the play, and the most probable
place for the interval in a stage production. That this effect was consciously

produced by O'Neill is evident from alterations he made to the first draft of the play, in which he cut away the original ending until these words were prominent. The parallelism of the phrases "so happy" / "so lonely" means that each calls the other to mind. It is no mistake that the final line of the play should be, "I fell in love with James Tyrone and was so happy for a time."

Mary's affliction, which makes a ghost or a fog person out of a flesh and blood human being, is the result of chance and circumstance and, as such, is a peculiarly powerful image through which O'Neill can project the tension between received ideas of order and experience of disorder, between faith and unwilled scepticism. On paper, Jamie Tyrone would seem to be one of the weaker elements of the play, his condition a paler version of his mother's, since alcohol is less strange to us than morphine, its effects less immediately drastic and its influence less clearly the result of accident or of a single blow of Fate. The characterization is more vulnerable to distortion in the event of any looseness on the part of the author because the audience are likely to have preconceptions about alcoholism which may sway them towards sympathy, sentimentality or hostility, making this figure seem less real than the other three. The characterization is similarly threatened by the traditional stage stereotypes of the charming wastrel and of the drunken buffoon. In the event, O'Neill demonstrates how complex Jamie is in contrast to the stage stereotypes and so draws the character as to leave no room for any private gloss by the audience. Jamie is as credible and as mysterious as the other three characters, and his presence is as essential in creating the fine balance which exists between them.

Jamie is presented as living a death-in-life but the "dead part" of him is responsible for his sharp tongue, from which much of the humour and vigour of the play derives. The audience, therefore, responding to his recitation, his jokes, his startling but frequently apt remarks about the other characters, finds itself drawn into partial collusion with him. Moreover, since a large part of the information about Jamie derives from the testimony of other characters which must be modified subsequently in the light of actual words and deeds, we are continually forced to recognize that he is more complex than the testimony allows. We are constantly confronted with the positive elements of a largely negative figure.

In the opening scene of the play, Jamie compliments his mother, laughs at his brother's joke, shrugs off his father's attacks, but actually says very little. What he does say is commonplace enough. The audience is thus alerted to the disparity between what they observe and the hypersensitivity of the other characters towards Jamie. Edmund is quick to notice and parry attacks on him; Mary becomes defensive when she catches him looking at her, Tyrone attacks him without noticeable provocation. Prompted by the testimony, we are led to see that Jamie's neutrality is a deliberate withdrawal from any demanding situation: "Let's forget it," "Oh, all right, I'm a fool to argue," "All right, Papa, I'm a bum. Anything you like so long as it stops the argument." If this seems to support Tyrone's opinion of his son's shiftlessness, the few times when Jamie does initiate the conversation present a different picture. In the atmosphere of mystification, we find that his impulse is towards the truth: "The Kid's damned sick," "I think it's the wrong idea to let Mama go on kidding herself," "He thinks it's consumption, doesn't he, Papa?" "God, this ought to be the one thing we can talk over frankly without a battle." When the promised sneers do come, therefore, late in act 1, the audience is prepared to find accuracy as well as malice in them. Their vigour is probably more surprising.

O'Neill couches Jamie's sneers in New York City slang drawing particularly on its habit of hyperbole and extravagant abuse: "If Edmund was a lousy acre of land you wanted, the sky would be the limit"; "I know it's an Irish peasant idea consumption is fatal. It probably is when you live in a hovel on a bog, but over here with modern treatment." His words are, therefore, projected forcefully, drawing our attention to the accuracy beneath the sneer. We begin to recognize that the other characters fear the sneers themselves less than the possibility that they represent the truth, and suspicion and appreciation conflict in our response to him. It is Rocky's rather than Harry Hope's kind of slang that Jamie usually speaks. We are conscious of the note of abuse even when no deliberate insult is intended. A man is "a louse," "a sap," "a boob," "a sucker," "a dumbell," living in a world of "hick burgs," "hooker shops," "cheap dumps" and talking "the bunk" or "drunken bull." At its lightest, the humour is uncomplimentary, achieving its effects through bathos, "I was half-way up the walk when Cathleen burst into song. Our wild Irish lark! She ought to be a train announcer," or derisive incongruity, "I shall attain the pinnacle of success! I'll be the lover of the fat woman in Barnum and Bailey's circus." But the slang usage is developed differently here from in the earlier play.

In *The Iceman Cometh*, the shared slang helped to reveal the communal feeling of Hope's roomers. This effect is now reversed. Jamie's slang indicates his alienation from his own home where no-one shares his language. His "foul tongue," his "rotten Broadway loafer's lingo" is specifically rejected by the other characters and the gulf is the wider because of the half-echo we find in Edmund's speech. The younger man occasionally adopts the lexis but never the spirit of the slang and it is from him that the sharpest repudiation of it comes in his scornful parody:

> They never come back! Everything is in the bag! It's all a frame-up! We're all fall guys and suckers and we can't beat the game! (. . .) Christ, if I felt the way you do—!

The other difference is that Jamie is not limited to a single variety of English. In the first act, slang words and attitudes are loosely interspersed with Standard and do not become persistent until after Mary's return to the drug. It is only rarely used with full force, but when it is then it is the kind of slang Bewley proscribed:

> no fresh language, but a tired, thin-blooded language, dead sophisticated in a popular way, and afraid to stop moving lest it should not easily get into motion again.
>
> > (*The Complex Fate*)

The shock of his sudden brutal coarseness, "Another shot in the arm!", "Where's the hop-head?", is reinforced by the response of the stage listeners, by Tyrone's anger and by Edmund's swift physical reflex action, as well as by Jamie's own subsequent collapse into silent sobs. When O'Neill wishes Jamie's words to carry conviction he uses no slang. To Tyrone's accusation that his son sneers at everyone except himself, Jamie replies, "You can't hear me talking to myself, that's all," and, in explanation of his bitterness towards his mother, "She thinks I always believe the worst, but this time I believed the best. I suppose I can't forgive her—yet. It meant so much." The simplicity of the language here gives the actor the cue to the tone in which they must be spoken. As so often in this play, it is the contrast with what occurs elsewhere which makes the particular words moving.

Jamie's absence during act 3 has a realistic explanation, but it is also strategic. He is removed at the point in time when his tongue, were he to remain on stage, must become most callous. His harshness is communicated by means of reported rather than direct speech and so is tempered. The references to Jamie are frequent but usually brief, "You say such mean bitter things when you've drunk too much. You're as bad as Jamie or Edmund"; "That loafer! I hope to God he misses the last car and has to stay up-town." Two are rather more extended: Mary in her reverie projects a picture of Jamie's childhood. There is no didacticism here because the information about Jamie is given almost by the way—our recognition of his early emotional deprivation is gleaned between the lines of Mary's telling of her own tragic experience of life. Edmund's discussion of Jamie in act 4 is more direct. He presents a hypothetical image of Jamie's actions off-stage at the moment of speaking. The presentation is ambivalent because Jamie's thought is satirized through the quotation of two poems with whose writers Edmund, only a short time before, has identified himself. Edmund's own position is again in question, as it was when he parodied Jamie's "lingo." We gather that the relationship between the brothers is less straightforward than either claims, and that the intimacy between the two can be betrayed by the younger as well as by the older. When Jamie enters, the reality of his action is superimposed on the image. Since image and reality almost coincide, our attention is fixed on the few differences. Jamie has indeed been reciting poetry to a fat whore in a brothel but his wry recognition of the humour in the situation shows us a self-knowledge greater than had been allowed. Where Edmund's account was narrated and generalized, Jamie's is particularized and delivered as a series of performances: Mamie beefing, Fat Vi giving a "grand bawling out," Jamie crying and sentimentalizing whilst conscious of the reactions of the onlooker. We find a vitality in the speech of the man, who is able to produce nothing, that is lacking in the words of the incipient writer. We find, too, that Jamie's deliberate selection of Fat Vi has been an act of impulsive sympathy towards another human being so that in this, as well, he has proved larger than the portrait.

If we are repeatedly made to feel that there is more to Jamie than meets the eye, we find that his younger brother continually eludes our grasp. Edmund's identity seems to be unformed rather than shifting like those of the other members of the family. He is ten years younger than Jamie, but seems a lifetime away from brother and parents because he is the only one for whom possibilities remain. He is the one link the Tyrones have with the future. He stands at that point in time to which Tyrone and Mary both look back and which Jamie can never experience. O'Neill casts a particularly dark shadow on this seemingly doomed family by making him the character whom tuberculosis will possibly kill.

O'Neill achieves this effect of Edmund's being not quite formed, not yet an adult, by emphasizing his clumsiness and enthusiasm. His eagerness to reassure Mary, at the end of act 1, is for her the signal of mistrust which finally pushes her back on the drug, whilst his inexperience and optimism make him slow to realize that she has returned to it, in act 2, scene 1. He is stoutly optimistic, but when he attempts to act on his hope, we see at once

that there is no substance to it. He cannot begin to talk on equal ground
with his mother. She manipulates him verbally in act 1, and avoids his
appeal in act 3. The awkwardness of his revolt against his father invites
comparison with Jamie's verbal dexterity. In reply to Tyrone's quotation
of Prospero, for example, Edmund rephrases Shakespeare's words:

> Fine! That's beautiful. But I wasn't trying to say that. We are
> such stuff as manure is made on, so let's drink up and forget it.
> That's more my idea.

We are aware that Jamie would never have been so rash as to rewrite
Shakespeare but would have parried Tyrone's optimism by silent scorn or
by the witty selection of another accurate quotation whose meaning would
be distorted by the context to reflect his cynicism. The contrast is telling
and warns us against too easily discussing the character's clumsiness as if it
were the dramatist's. Edmund's inexperience is revealed, too, when his
sensitivity to the response of the outside world breaks through incongru-
ously at moments when private grief would be expected to be uppermost.
It is the character who in the bright morning had declared in support of
Tyrone's independent attitude, "He's right not to give a damn what
anyone thinks. Jamie's a fool to care about the Chatfields . . . whoever
heard about them outside this hick burg?", who later cries to his mother,
"For God's sake, Mama! You can't trust her! Do you want everyone on
earth to know?" and says to his father:

> to think when it's a question of your son having consumption,
> you can show yourself up before the whole town as such a
> stinking old tightwad! Don't you know Hardy will talk and the
> while damned town will know?

When he is not talking a great deal, as in his narration of the joke in act 1
or during the vigil he shares with Tyrone in act 4, he talks noticeably little.
Indeed, of his eighty-five separate utterances in acts 2 and 3, sixty-three
consist of only one or two terse sentences or half sentences, and only nine
of five or more sentences. Since it is in these acts that the family afflictions
become apparent, this brevity helps to indicate the difficulty he finds in
coping with the situation. Many of his utterances are appeals to the others
for silence, "Cut it out, Papa"; "Don't, mother"; "Stop talking, Mama."
And, of all the characters, it is he who resorts most often to gesture
because words have failed him. He twice attacks Jamie physically and once

recollects having done so and in his misery at the end of act 3, he runs out to hide himself in the fog.

We catch echoes of all the other characters in Edmund's speech: of Jamie's slang, Mary's vocabulary, Tyrone's delight in the sound of words. He adopts Jamie's slang, for instance, particularly in conversation with or about his brother, but his usage is woolly. Expressions like, "Nix on the loud noise"; "Don't look at me as though I'd gone nutty," lack the callousness but also the pungency of Jamie's idiom. They are sufficient to indicate both the influence of brother on brother and the limits of that influence.

The characterization is not as negative as my discussion so far suggests. What at one moment we call "unformed," at the next we might describe as "not fixed." His retreat from the word might equally be seen as self-assertion through physical action. His sensitivity to the situation implies a degree of feeling not hardened by habit. Although the other characters fear Jamie's tongue, the most cutting comments on the situation come from the lips of the naïve son. His mockery of Jamie's melancholy self-analysis stops his brother short; his appeal at the end of the play, almost impinges on Mary and it is he who shows Tyrone that his symbol of the past is to be equated with Mary's when, in what is in its implications one of the cruellest lines of the play, he suggests that Booth's praise for Tyrone's Othello "might be in an old trunk in the attic, along with Mama's wedding dress."

One sequence in Edmund's utterance demands detailed attention for it is one that has been praised as poetic and denounced as embarrassing. It seems to me to be a scene in which the difference in the dramatist's control between the first and second parts of his career is clearly evinced.

We have seen that in the first part of his career, O'Neill adopted a heightened form of language, notable for its flowing rhythm, in passages of reverie, of confession or of recollection of the past. It was sometimes effective, as when Anna Christie dreamed in the fog or Orin Mannon brooded about the battlefield but, almost always, it was out of key with the rest of the play—an interlude in the action, not an integral part of it. There is no equivalent passage in *The Iceman Cometh*. Larry Slade's speech breaks down when he begins to probe his own consciousness and, in Hickey's confession, O'Neill emphasizes speech rhythms, making use of the parentheses, redundancies and syntactical irregularities of talk. The confessions of Tyrone and Jamie, in act 4 of *Long Day's Journey into Night*, follow this pattern. They are idiomatic rather that lyrical. And Mary's reverie is cast into an idiosyncratic form which is an extension of one of her habitual speech rhythms. But what are we to make of Edmund's confession? The character based on the young O'Neill uses the register we have identified with O'Neill's personal voice to recount an experience of ecstasy. Not surprisingly, Edmund's comment on the passage has been taken as O'Neill's assessment of his own work and discussion has usually centered on the statement "it will be faithful realism, at least. Stammering is the native eloquence of us fog people." This has led to the divorce of the passage from its context and the subsequent discussion of its merits as literary prose in isolation from its dramatic function.

The passage does read awkwardly but to label it an unfortunate patch in an otherwise well-written play and then pass on, will not do. It occupies a long stretch of performance time at a crucial moment of the play and if it did not contribute positively to the ongoing action, it would damage it badly. Since experience of performance suggests that there is no such damage here, it is necessary to consider whether it could succeed as dramatic dialogue whilst failing as literary prose.

It is necessary to quote a rather longer sequence than usually suffices and, even then, it is important to remember that the scene modifies and is modified by previous and subsequent scenes. Edmund speaks to his father:

> Yes, she moves above and beyond us, a ghost haunting the past, and here we sit pretending to forget, but straining our ears listening for the slightest sound, hearing the fog drip from the eaves like the uneven tick of a rundown, crazy clock—or like the dreary tears of a trollop spattering in a puddle of stale beer on a honky-tonk table top! (*He laughs with maudlin appreciation.*) Not so bad, that last, eh? Original, not Baudelaire. Give me credit! (*Then with alcoholic talkativeness.*) You've just told me some high spots in your memories. Want to hear mine? They're all connected with the sea. Here's one. When I was on the squarehead square-rigger, bound for Buenos Aires. Full moon in the Trades. The old hooker driving fourteen knots. I lay on the bowsprit, facing astern, with the water foaming into spume under me, the masts with every sail white in the moonlight, towering high above me. I became drunk with the beauty and singing rhythm of it, and for a moment I lost myself— actually lost my life. I was set free! I dissolved in the sea, became white sails and flying spray, became beauty and rhythm, became moonlight and the ship and the high dim-

starred sky! I belonged, without past or future, within peace and unity and a wild joy, within something greater than my own life, or the life of Man, to Life itself! To God, if you want to put it that way. Then another time, on the American Line, when I was lookout on the crow's nest in the dawn watch. A calm sea, that time. Only a lazy ground swell and a slow drowsy roll of the ship. The passengers asleep and none of the crew in sight. No sound of man. Black smoke pouring from the funnels behind and beneath me. Dreaming, not keeping lookout, feeling alone, and above, and apart, watching the dawn creep like a painted dream over the sky and sea which slept together. Then the moment of ecstatic freedom came. The peace, the end of the quest, the last harbour, the joy of belonging to a fulfilment beyond men's lousy, pitiful, greedy fears and hopes and dreams! And several other times in my life, when I was swimming far out, or lying alone on a beach, I have had the same experience. Became the sun, the hot sand, green seaweed anchored to a rock, swaying in the tide. Like a saint's vision of beatitude. Like the veil of things as they seem drawn back by an unseen hand. For a second you see—and seeing the secret, are the secret. For a second there is meaning! Then the hand lets the veil fall and you are alone, lost in the fog again, and you stumble on toward nowhere, for no good reason! (*He grins wryly.*) It was a great mistake my being born a man, I would have been much more successful as a sea-gull or a fish. As it is, I will always be a stranger who never feels at home, who does not really want and is not really wanted, who can never belong, who must always be a little in love with death!

TYRONE (*stares at him—impressed*). Yes, there's the makings of a poet in you all right. (*Then protesting uneasily.*) But that's morbid craziness about not being wanted and loving death.

EDMUND (*sardonically*). The *makings* of a poet. No, I'm afraid I'm like the guy who is always panhandling for a smoke. He hasn't even got the makings. He's got only the habit. I couldn't touch what I tried to tell you just now. I just stammered. That's the best I'll ever do. I mean if I live.

Well it will be faithful realism, at least. Stammering is the
native eloquence of us fog people.
(*A pause. Then they both jump startledly as there is a noise
from outside the house, as if someone had stumbled and
fallen on the front steps. Edmund grins.*)
Well, that sounds like the absent brother. He must have a
peach of a bun on.

Unlike such passages in the earlier plays, the reverie here is set within a
frame. The speaker introduces and afterwards comments on it, so that
attention is directed towards the efforts of the nascent poet to express his
experience as well as towards the experience itself. The somewhat bizarre
sentence with which the passage begins, and with sixty-five words it is the
longest in the play, takes us, at the outset, past the meaning to the mode of
expression. The vague, literary description of Mary in the opening clause
gives way to an accurate observation of the present ("here we sit, pretending to forget, but straining our ears listening for the slightest sound").
This, in its turn, is diffused by the comparison between the fog and the
"rundown, crazy clock" which, somewhat awkward, distracts the audience's attention to itself. What establishes the difference between the effect
of this and of similar stylistic mixtures in the middle plays is that the
dramatist, conscious now of the impression created, is able to use it. The
elaborate description of the clock appears to distract the speaker, too,
from his meaning to his style so that he ends the sentence with the
exuberant anticlimax of "or like the dreary tears of a trollop spattering in
a puddle of stale beer on a honky-tonk table top!," and then adds the
self-conscious comment, "Not bad that last, eh? Original, not Baudelaire."
The experience of ecstasy is introduced equally self-consciously ("Want to
hear mine? Here's one"), and is punctuated by prosaic reminders that a
speaker is communicating with a listener ("Then another time . . . And
several other times"). The description of the scene ("Full moon in the
Trades," "the high dim-starred sky," "watching the dawn creep"), and the
thought ("I belonged to Life itself," "belonging to a fulfilment," "you see
and seeing the secret, are the secret") tell us little about the experience, as
do the literary echoes we catch (of Dana in the sequence about the
bowsprit, Wordsworth in the references to "wild joy" and "unity," and
Shelley in the image of the veil). The descriptive passages are clichés and
unfocused abstractions, whilst the literary echoes, reminding us of the
greater coherence of the source, are disturbing rather than illuminating.
But, because of the frame which encloses them—the speaker's self-

consciousness—both descriptions and echoes lead us to the character and not, as they did in the middle plays, to the struggling dramatist.

O'Neill uses the literary effusiveness of his own late adolescence for purposes of characterization. A play could not bear many such passages, but it can bear this one because of the support given by the surrounding dialogue and its consistency with what we have learnt of the character. We find in it, Edmund's clumsiness, his enthusiasm, and his delight in the words of poets. The word-play of the "dreary tears of the trollop" sequence, with its pattern of plosive consonants, has a disarming excess, of a kind we meet again. Images are taken too far ("became the sun, the hot sand, the green seaweed anchored to a rock swaying in the tide") and nouns, adjectives or adverbs tumble over each other in the eagerness of expression ("feeling alone, above, and apart," "Men's lousy, pitiful, greedy fears and hopes and dreams"). Although verbally imprecise, the passage has a rhythmic coherence. The medley of ideas in that opening sentence, for example, are bound together by the repeated use of the continuous present form of the verb ("haunting . . . pretending . . . straining . . . listening . . . hearing . . . spattering"). And in the reverie itself, which moves from the past tense ("When I was") through the present ("for a second you see") to the continuous form of the future ("I will always"), the separate sentences are bound into larger periods by patterning. In Edmund's first sea memory, for instance, each of four consecutive long sentences is introduced by a first person pronoun and a simple past tense ("I lay . . . I became . . . I dissolved . . . I belonged"). Within the first two sentences, ideas are grouped in pairs, within the second, they are arranged in sets of three, associated by the reiteration of the verb in one set ("I dissolved . . . *became* white sails and flying spray, *became* beauty and rhythm, *became* moonlight and"), of the preposition in the other ("I belonged, *without* past or future, *within* peace and unity and a wild joy, *within* something greater"). Attention is focused on the climax of this first vision because the rolling sentences are replaced by a sudden brief one, "To God, if you want to put it that way." The audience, swept along by the rhythm and by the boyish voice speaking into the silence in an urgent tone, is likely to concur with Tyrone's comment, "Yes there's the makings of a poet in you all right." But as soon as the utterance ceases qualifications will begin to flood in. Our recognition that we have been led by the rhythm and the enthusiasm to a spurious response is immediately absorbed by O'Neill into the action of the play when, in the coda to Edmund's utterance, the qualifications are put into the character's own mouth in language that breaks the pattern. A precise image and a wry pun phrased in earthy slang replace the abstractions, and short, disjointed sentences replace the rhythmic flow. The recognition of failure is spoken in a direct, unfurbished statement, "I couldn't touch what I tried to tell you just now." O'Neill makes us aware of the gulf between longing and capacity and confronts us at a more complex level with that area of human experience he explored in *Desire under the Elms*. Like the early patterned use of the word "purty," Edmund's reverie with its plain-speaking coda makes us conscious not only of his inarticulacy but of his pain at being unable to articulate his deeply felt experience. It is this pain which activates the private emotions of the audience.

If we also catch a reference to the dramatist's private experience in the "stammering" comment, the frisson we feel helps to intensify the response much as happens if we seem to hear Shakespeare's voice speaking with Prospero's in the "Our revels now are ended" speech in *The Tempest*. If we return to the speech after the play to seek out the writer, we find a nice irony in the fact that one of O'Neill's most memorable lines in a play in which he is so fully master of his form should have been written about his verbal infelicity. But, in the play, such consciousness could only be fleeting because Jamie is heard entering and seriousness gives way to the farce of the drunken man stumbling in the fog of his inebriation. Our viewpoint is already being shifted and new impressions are modifying those just made. Edmund's clumsy slang, "He must have a peach of a bun on," reminds us that he is also a novice in Jamie's world where, if metaphors are inappropriate, they are deliberately and grotesquely so. The audience themselves feel the edge of Jamie's cynicism because it is directed against the moment of intimacy just witnessed between Edmund and Tyrone, which has seemed one of the few wholly positive exchanges in the play: "He's been putting on the old sob act for you, eh? He can always kid you. But not me. Never again." And, before long, the mood has darkened again with the third and cruellest of the self-exposures in which Jamie, in his turn, achieves his own kind of stammering eloquence.

C.W.E. BIGSBY

Four Early Plays

*B*eyond the Horizon (1920) marked O'Neill's Broadway début. It was his first play performed by a professional cast and presented by a major commercial producer and when it received the Pulitzer prize in 1921 he had clearly staked his claim as America's leading young playwright.

The play is the story of two brothers: one, Robert, a dreamer who wishes to go to sea, to encounter the world beyond the horizon, the other, Andrew, a practical farmer for whom the daily routine of farm life provides meaning enough. But both men love the same girl. And when, to everyone's surprise, she chooses the dreamer, he relinquishes his place on his uncle's boat and decides to stay on the farm, while his brother, bitter at having lost her, goes to sea. The marriage proves disastrous. Robert is no farmer and the decline of the marriage and of the farm are conterminous. Eventually he dies of tuberculosis, his body as emaciated as his spirit. With his dying breath he asks his brother, physically fit but morally damaged, to take his place. With his remaining strength he drags himself out onto the road and dies looking at the horizon that he had never managed to transcend.

Beyond the Horizon is, in effect, a portrait of O'Neill's own warring instincts. One brother is drawn to the practical world. He is unimaginative, creative only to the extent that he has the will to dominate his circumstances and imprint his identity on a world with which he is at harmony. The other is a delicately featured dreamer, prone to consump-

From *Twentieth-Century American Drama, 1900–1940,* vol. 1. © 1982 by Cambridge University Press.

tion, cowed by the environment which he allows to dominate him. The one constructs the world out of fact, the other out of pure imagination. But both betray themselves, wilfully going against their natural instincts—a fact unnecessarily underscored by O'Neill. For when Andrew destroys his harmonious relationship with the land by becoming a property speculator O'Neill has his brother spell out the moral: "You used to be a creator when you loved the farm. You and life were in harmonious partnership. And now . . . You—a farmer—to gamble in a wheat pit with scraps of paper. There's a spiritual significance in that picture." Indeed! But the significance lies in an action which has no need of explication.

The other brother, Robert, has equally betrayed his creative gifts, marrying on impulse (reminiscent of O'Neill's own marriage) and abandoning his dreams, subordinating his talents to the simple determinants of daily existence. Like so many of O'Neill's characters he is obsessed with the constrictions which fate—expressed through character and environment—has placed around him. The hills surrounding the farm become "like the walls of a narrow prison yard shutting" him "in from all the freedom and wonder of life"; the house, a place where he had been "cooped" up. His daughter dies from inherited consumption. Life is a process of disillusion, of disintegration, manifested in a loss of control over physical being (the ravages of time on the various characters are stressed by O'Neill in his stage directions and constitute evidence of dissolution) and the decay evidenced by the setting itself, which expresses a sense of exhaustion. And though this suffering is offered as a form of grace by the dying Robert, the final stage direction suggests a sense of stasis from which recovery is impossible. For Ruth is too debilitated, physically and spiritually, to be redeemed by a suffering which has simply brutalised and not ennobled. She remains silent "with the sad humility of exhaustion, her mind already sinking back into that spent calm beyond the further troubling of any hope."

O'Neill was, as he said in a letter to the critic Arthur Hobson Quinn, "always acutely aware of the reality and power of determinism" but he wished to view this in the context of a tragic vision which could transform that determinism. As he said shortly after the premiere of *Beyond the Horizon*, which had been hailed as an American tragedy (and even by one critic as the first modern native tragedy), "It is the meaning of life—and the hope. The noblest is eternally the most tragic. The people who succeed and do not push on to greater failure are the spiritual middle classes. Their stopping at success is proof of their compromising insignificance. How petty their dreams must have been." But it is hard to see how this statement can be said to apply to *Beyond the Horizon*. The failure of the characters derives not from the greatness of their dreams, or even the courage with which they tackle a task imposed by fate. It is a consequence of their capitulation to biological impulse, of their capacity for self-destruction, of their wilful abandonment of dreams for immediate satisfactions of one kind or another. The potential spiritual unity which both brothers, in their different ways, glimpse is abruptly and arbitrarily aborted by a fate in which the heavy hand of the playwright becomes a simple extension of a romantic sense of inevitable doom. The setting is, in effect, Hardy's dark star. The game is so thoroughly rigged and so precipitately enacted that the concept of moral authority, of a resistant self, of a courageous challenging of the determined, makes no sense. The self is too thoroughly infected, literally and symbolically, for it to sustain a tragic mode. The one brother fails in large part because his strength is taken away by disease, the other because, removed from our attention, character is arbitrarily changed to permit him to betray a nature laboriously established earlier in the play. Suffering implies a grace but it is a grace which remains unexamined and which is unconvincing.

For Nietzsche, the problem of the meaning of suffering resolved itself into a Christian or Dionysian one. As he explained in *The Will to Power* "In the former case it is to be the way toward holy being, in the latter, being itself is holy enough to justify an enormity of suffering . . . The god on the cross is a curse on life, pointing to a redemption from life. Dionysus, torn to pieces, is a promise of life—it will be eternally reborn and return again from destruction." In *Beyond the Horizon* the ideas are confused. Robert simultaneously invokes a Christian version of redemption through pain, and a Dionysian encomium on life. He looks forward to the next world, while recalling the purity of his original vision. But he capitulates, finally, to a Christian and hence non-tragic perception and by doing so ensnares his brother in the same anti-life vortex from which death alone has rescued him. He bequeaths his wife to a brother who is now tied to his fate by a moral imperative which leaves no room for an expansive soul. Prosaic himself, he must now mortgage his future to a woman drained of all energy, vision and hope. The play ends not on tragic but an ironic note: hence the division among the reviewers who called it, on the one hand, tragic, and on the other, gloomy. The world of *Beyond the Horizon* is essentially that of Nietzsche's madman alter ego in *The Gay Science* who identified a world in which a sponge had wiped "away the whole horizon," a world through which the individual strayed, "an infinite nothing" feeling "the breath of empty space."

If *Beyond the Horizon* established O'Neill's popular reputation, there is little doubt that his finest and most original play in these early years was *The Emperor Jones* (1920). It opened to almost universally approving notices and, despite occasional baffled allusion to tragedy, O'Neill having successfully planted the idea of his tragic intent in reviewers' minds, it was in fact a brilliantly original account of a disintegrating private and public world.

His dramatic strategy in the play lay in the deconstruction of character, in the dismantling of social forms and the unhinging of language. Assurance about the substantiality of the self, the sequentiality of history and the subordinate nature of event and environment crumbles under pressure. The collapse is not simply atavism of a kind which might make the play racially suspect. His concern is with dramatising an unconscious whose irrationalisms are ultimately the generators of meaning and the expressions of an anarchy within, which the conscious mind is designed to suppress. Here, the desire for order and the awareness of the world's refusal to render any coherence beyond the ultimate stasis of death are dramatised within the individual. The irony is self-contained.

Brutus Jones, an American Negro who has escaped from America where he had committed two murders, finds himself on an island in the West Indies "as yet not self-determined by White Mariners." (The capitalisation implies a level of social criticism which the play never really takes up.) By dint of judiciously pandering to local superstitions, he quickly establishes himself as Emperor and begins salting away money. He protects himself from assassination by asserting that he can only be killed by a silver bullet. When the play begins, however, a rebellion is already under way and Jones begins a prepared retreat through the tropical forest, with the sound of drums in his ears. Once in the forest his social assurance collapses. He abandons his clothes, fires his revolver at his own formless fears and memories as they materialise in the darkness, and is ultimately killed by a silver bullet specially prepared by the natives, whose spells may or may not have liberated the anarchic spirits which in fact destroy him. The final remark of the play, delivered by Henry Smithers, a cockney trader who has profited from Jones's seizure of power, is singularly inappropriate. His observation that the natives are "stupid as 'ogs, the lot of 'em! Blasted niggers!" is a sign of his failure to understand what he has seen.

On one level the play is clearly a comment on imperialism, as it is an assault on the more obvious presumptions of racism. Its observations on the mercenary motives and coercive methods of government, its identification of that government's method of enforcing its power through the manipulation of opinion and through capitalising on prejudice, its suggestion that government is in effect a criminal enterprise, are clear enough. But the play is not primarily a satire. Its basic concern is with exposing the unconscious, dramatising the imagination, tapping the anarchic truths, the discontinuities of the mind. Below the level of narrative is a contraflow of images destabilising the surface. Past and present mix. Sequence defers to simultaneity as the nodal points of personal and race history coalesce. Character fragments into pulses of experience, alternating fears and certainties. It is a play of considerable originality—a genuine achievement which showed the real resources of a playwright whose territory was the mind and its conflicts rather than the social world. The mise-en-scène itself becomes a character—the forest trees closing around Jones, expressions of the terror that suffocates and immobilises him.

And yet there is a version of history unfolded here. For the memories that well up into Jones's consciousness are not only of events which he had experienced. They are race memories derived from a history of oppression. He sees a vision of a slave auction in the 1850s, a fiction into which he is drawn, becoming himself the object of the sale. He reenacts the experience of the voyage to America on board a slave ship, joining his voice with that of the other slaves in a wail of agony as they experience the roll of the ship (some fifty years later Amiri Baraka also tried to forge a theatrical ritual out of the same material). Ultimately Jones finds himself the victim of a pagan ritual sacrifice—a Jungian dramatisation of race consciousness and of an archetypal experience.

Indeed, the play seems to bring together and develop in parallel a personal unconscious and a collective unconscious. As Jung was later to explain in an essay entitled, "The concept of the collective unconscious:"

> the collective unconscious is part of the psyche which can be negatively distinguished from a personal unconscious by the fact that it does not owe its existence to personal experience and consequently is not a personal acquisition. While the personal unconscious is made up essentially of contents which have at one time been conscious but which have disappeared from consciousness through having been forgotten or repressed, the contents of the collective unconscious have never been in consciousness, and therefore have never been individually acquired, but owe their existence exclusively to heredity. Whereas the personal unconscious consists for the most part of *com-*

plexes, the content of the collective unconscious is made up essentially of archetypes.

The archetype, as Jung indicates, is what Adolf Bastian, perhaps more tellingly in this context, had called "primordial thoughts."

In the final vision/experience which Jones undergoes in O'Neill's play a witch-doctor enacts a ritual, a play within a play, which comments on the experience which Jones is himself going through:

> The WITCH-DOCTOR sways, stamping with his foot, his bone rattle clicking the time. His voice rises and falls in a weird, monotonous croon, without articulate word divisions. Gradually his dance becomes clearly one of a narrative in pantomime demanding sacrifice. He flees, he is pursued by devils, he flees again. Ever weaker and wilder becomes his flight, nearer and nearer draws the pursuing evil, more and more the spirit of terror gains possession of him.

The collapse of language creates rather than destroys meaning. All the images from the past are presented in mime. The process of pressing back into the past towards pre-history is a process of dispensing with language. It is also presented as a move towards truth—simultaneously a Freudian and a theatrical assertion of the primacy of non-verbal communication. At the level of language lies are possible; at the level of instinctual behaviour, of gesture, and of unconscious impulse there is an available truth. By the same token the accretions of 'civilisation' have served merely to obscure this truth. Language has become the agent of exploitation, identity a disguise to facilitate theft. The conscious world is a world of deceit, of deliberate obfuscation.

O'Neill sets himself the task of penetrating an equal mystery—the unconscious roots of action—precisely the world which Macgowan and Jones were urging as the real subject of the modern dramatist in their books on theatre. As Freud said, in an essay called "The unconscious and consciousness" (1901–2), "The unconscious is the true psychological reality; *in its innermost nature it is as much unknown to us as the reality of the external world, and it is as incompletely presented by the data of consciousness as is the external world by the communications of our sense organs.*" But for Emperor Jones there is no distinction. The membrane dividing real from unreal, conscious from unconscious dissolves. The superstitions of the natives seem successfully to have invaded his mind.

Hence their sense of triumph at the end of the play, as they believe themselves to have defeated him. But Freud himself had described superstition as *"nothing but psychology projected into the external world."* Indeed, he sought a parallel in paranoia for the process whereby psychical factors are mirrored in "the construction of a supernatural reality." And, of course, *The Emperor Jones* is a study of a paranoid individual as it is an observation about the psychopathology of a group. Jones's reactions are readily explicable in Freudian terms. His superstition is not only a race memory, a trace element of history. It is explicable in clinical terms. For Freud, superstition "is in large part the expiation of trouble; and a person who has harboured frequent evil wishes against others, but has been brought up to be good and has therefore suppressed such wishes into the unconscious, will be especially ready to expect punishment for his unconscious wickedness in the form of trouble threatening him from without."

The Emperor Jones (1920) was a startlingly innovative play. O'Neill later objected to those who saw it primarily as a Freudian work, and certainly its force lies elsewhere than simply in its account of repressed guilts. Like Strindberg in his last plays, O'Neill discovered with *The Emperor Jones* the plasticity of the stage, deconstructing its new-found solidities alongside his dislocation of character, language and plot. He discovered, what Robert Edmond Jones was to assert in his book on *The Dramatic Imagination*, that the setting was potentially "a presence, a mood, a warm wind fanning the drama to flame. It echoes, it enhances, it animates. It is an expectancy, a foreboding, a tension." Likewise his use of sound. In the sea plays he had experimented with contrapuntal rhythms which were expressive on the one hand of the natural world of the natives and on the other of the degraded and disjointed world of the sailors. Now he uses sound, throughout the play, in the form of a drumbeat which is offered as a resonant correlative of Jones's pulse, a blood rhythm not to be denied by time or by evasive role-playing. The continual throb of the tom-tom—a projection of Jones's heartbeat which ceases abruptly with his life—emphasises another of the play's themes, the slow process of deconstruction which is the process of life itself. For Jones's physical and mental collapse provides a foreshortened, temporally collapsed, version of the entropic process of mortality.

Three years later O'Neill returned to the question of race and regressive pressures of the social world. *All God's Chillun Got Wings* (1924) describes the relationship between a black man and a white woman. As children they had been largely free of prejudice, using the language of racism but drained of real meaning. Like most of O'Neill's early work, the setting is claustrophobic, with tenements closing around the figures who in some senses become mere extrusions of their environment—in this case an environment rigidly divided along racial lines. The mechanical rhythms of the street are an image of the mechanical lives of those who exist in the constricting boundaries of the city. To cross boundaries of any kind is to invite suspicion. When Jim Harris wishes to become a lawyer this is seen as an act of defection by his fellow blacks. "What's all dis dressin' up and graduatin' an' sayin' you gwine study to be a lawyer? What's all dis fakin' an' pretendin' an' swellin' out grand an' talkin' soft and perlite? What all dis denyin' you's a nigger ... Tell me befo' I wrecks yo' face in! Is you a nigger or isn't you? Is you a nigger, nigger?" So powerful are the myths of colour that Jim is unable to deal with the effortless superiority of whites, internalising their values and unconsciously accepting their assertions of his inadequacy. Even the desire to succeed as a lawyer is a sign that he has accepted the values of the society he struggles to join. The passing of the examinations will enable him to "pass" as white, not because he has a white skin but because his language, his appearance and his values will be those of white society. The effort is simultaneously legitimate aspiration and a fundamental betrayal of himself—a perception which in some ways makes O'Neill close kin to those black dramatists of the 1960s who made a similar point. Jim believes that he must pass the examinations before he can claim Ella, the white girl, as his wife—indeed he is doubtful whether he can ever aspire to that status, being content to live in her shadow. But she is equally trapped in her own myths. Though used and abused by a callous white man she is ambivalent about Jim. She both loves and despises him and the pressures drive her to psychosis as equally they lead Jim to physical and mental breakdown. As in *The Emperor Jones*, O'Neill is concerned with the disintegration of personality, the subordination of the individual to history and to myth. And once again the mise-en-scène becomes an actor in the drama—not merely with respect to the racially divided streets but more especially with regard to the primitive Negro mask which hangs on the wall of Jim's apartment and which becomes the embodiment of the social prejudices which Ella has absorbed.

The fact of race taunts her as it does Jim. They try to escape the dilemma by running to Europe but are pursued by it. And, as in *The Emperor Jones*, the physical world seems to shrink, compressing them to the point at which character is reduced to type and the space for social action is destroyed. The stage directions indicate that "The walls of the room appear shrunken in, the ceiling lowered, so that the furniture, the portrait, the mask, look unnaturally large and domineering." Jim wants to break out of his constraints, not to see his life in terms of history and myth. "You with your fool talk of the black race and the white race!" he objects to his sister, "Where does the human race get a chance to come in? I suppose that's simple for you. You lock it up in asylums and throw away the key." But this, of course, is exactly what does happen as both the principal characters are driven to the point of breakdown. And so they reenact the only period in which the schizophrenia of race had been inoperative—childhood. The adult world must be rejected. Sexuality must be denied. Career must be abandoned in favour of a pre-lapsarian world. Ella, who has been almost literally consumed by hatred, by self-contempt and by remorse, is reduced to a frail figure, her womanhood withered and denied. She is saved, paradoxically, only by Jim's failure to establish his adult status by graduating as a lawyer. His failure is ambiguous. In one sense it reestablishes the ordered world in which racial roles are paradigms of metaphysical purpose; it reasserts the constancy which she desperately wishes to cling to. But on the other hand it isolates them in a childlike innocence. As O'Neill indicates in a stage direction, she can at last freely kiss him but "she kisses his hand as a child might, tenderly and gratefully." And Jim joins her in this new innocence by falling on his knees and embracing the religion which is equally a product of an innocent world.

It is an apparently sentimental ending with a fierce undertow of irony. It is also, once again, an ending consonant with Freudian theory, for Freud observed, in his essay "The horror of incest," that "a neurotic . . . exhibits some degree of psychical infantilism." Indeed Jim and Ella are actually described as having lived "like friends—like a brother and sister." O'Neill clearly sees the pressures of race as having created this neurosis. For as Freud says of the neurotic, "He has either failed to get free from the psychosexual conditions that prevailed in his childhood or he has returned to them—two possibilities which may be summed up as developmental inhibition and regression." Intimidated by myths of racism Jim never considers himself an apt sexual partner for Ella. He offers himself as a friend, indeed as a worshipper. He is, in other words, from the beginning an example of "developmental inhibition," socially created.

But O'Neill was conscious that race was not the only prejudice with the power to warp the sensibility. As he insisted, "the Negro question, which, it must be remembered, is not an issue in the play, isn't the only one which can arouse prejudice. We are divided by prejudices. Prejudices racial, social, religious. Tracing it, it all goes back, of course, to economic causes." The "of course" is expressed in the play only through the oppressive nature of the tenement buildings but it is indicative of O'Neill's cast of

thought, his early plays generating poetic images of a human unity dis-
rupted by the forces of capitalism. The play's title is ironic. It is only in
heaven that freedom can be reality—hence Jim's reversion to a simplistic
faith at the end of the play. In the words of the spiritual from which the
title is derived:

> When I get to Heav'n
> Gonna put on my wings
> Gonna fly all over God's Heav'n.

In this world such freedom is not so readily available. Metaphysical
absurdities are compounded by social absurdities. It is a mark of O'Neill's
social iconoclasm that he should tackle the question of race, forging from
it a powerful metaphor of alienation in a play which takes a naturalistic
setting and exerts an expressionistic pressure on it of a kind which parallels the social pressure exerted on his protagonists. The walls of the
tenement close in on the fatal couple as do the walls of prejudice and
myth. The light changes from the brilliant glow of the setting sun on a hot
spring day to that of an arc lamp which "discovers faces with a favourless
cruelty." The growth from childhood to maturity becomes a moral regression. The bright faces and laughter of the children disappears. "There is no
laughter from the two streets," O'Neill tells us. The faces have begun to
distort. The collapse of style is a correlative of the collapse of individual
and human purpose.

For Kenneth Macgowan and Robert Edmond Jones, O'Neill was *the*
American expressionist, and the play which best exemplified his expressionist impulse was *The Hairy Ape*. Indeed, in a review in *Theatre Arts*,
Macgowan hailed it as the first American expressionist play, ignoring the
expressionist achievement of *The Emperor Jones*. Not surprisingly, but
also not at all accurately, the reviewer of *Industrial Solidarity* saw it as one
of the most helpful and legitimate defenses of the IWW (International
Workers of the World) position. Even Mike Gold attacked Heywood
Broun for failing to recognise the social reality in the play. But in truth the
alienation that lies at the heart of the play is more fundamental than most
reviewers were prepared to grant, while the clash between rich and poor
which seemed to lie at the heart of a profoundly social drama was in fact
simply further evidence of a sense of incompletion, of displacement which
lies at the heart of most of his work.

The Hairy Ape (1922) is a play about alienation. The ship, which
stands as a central image of society, sails aimlessly, its only function to

give pleasure to the wealthy who in fact find very little pleasure in it. It is on one level clearly a bitter social indictment—a satire on the vacuous world of the rich, and the soulless existence of the poor. But the prime value is not the need to revolt but to "belong." Indeed this is the only value which Yank, leader of the stokers in the boiler room, can identify. There is no ideology, no real communal sense which can claim their allegiance. Sexuality has been displaced. Masculinity now goes into the service of the machine which becomes a substitute for a life-giving feminine principle. And so Yank urges on his fellow stokers, as they feed the furnaces, in a language which is deliberately sexually suggestive: "Dat's de stuff! Let her have it! All togedder now! Sling it into her! Let her ride! Shoot de piece now! Call de toin on her. Drive her into it! Feel her move!" But no sooner does he cry out "Dere she go-o-es" than the voracious appetite of the machine demands their attention again. "We had a rest. Come on, she needs it! Give her pep!"

The image of misplaced sexuality becomes a dominant image of the 1920s in the work of Pound, Eliot, Lewis, Fitzgerald and Hemingway. And for O'Neill it operates as a symbol of the reductive power of a modern world in which the individual is always alienated from himself, from his fellow man and from his environment. Like Elmer Rice, he dramatises man as a machine. The stokers' voices have "a brazen, metallic quality as if their throats were phonograph horns." But the rich are equally mechanical. When Yank confronts them they appear nothing more than "a procession of gaudy marionettes, yet with something of the relentless horror of Frankensteins in their detached, mechanical unawareness." The real force which opposes this is not so much the "Wobblies" (International Workers of the World), who are seen as setting their faces against injustice, as the lyric reminders of a past world in which man was in tune with the natural world—a world celebrated by the old Irishman, Paddy, who recalls the "fine beautiful ships" and the "fine strong men in them . . . for we was free men . . . 'Twas them days men belonged to ships, not now. 'Twas them days a ship was part of the sea, and a man was part of a ship, and the sea joined all together and made it one." The unity has been destroyed by a selfishness which Yank and the débutante alike epitomise.

Mildred Douglas and her aunt are described as being conspicuously out of time with the natural world which is the setting but not home for figures who are described as being "two incongruous, artificial figures, inert and disharmonious" in contrast to the "beautiful, vivid life of the sea all about." If Yank's vitality is misdirected, sapped by the mechanical demands of the modern, Mildred betrays the fact that the vitality of her

stock had been sapped before she was conceived, so that she is the expression
not of its life energy but merely of the "artificialities that energy has won
for itself in the spending." The weakness of the play lies in the fact that
O'Neill feels it necessary to make Mildred state explicitly what is apparent
in the play's action, and in the images which he deploys. The reiterated
references to Yank's ape-like appearance, the insistence on the aridity and
inhumanity of the rich press the allegorical dimension too hard.

Yet the play transcends the social terms it erects. Confronted by the
Wobblies who find him as impossible to incorporate in their schema as
does Mildred in hers, Yank characterises their stance as a conviction that if
they can "cut an hour offen de job a day' they would 'make me happy!
Gimme a dollar more a day and make me happy! Tree square a day, and
cauliflowers in de front yard—an ekal rights—a woman and kids—a
lousey vote—and I'm all fixed for Jesus, huh?" Yank's alienation goes
much deeper. "It's way down—at de bottom. Yuh can't grab it, and yuh
can't stop it. It moves, an everyting moves. It stops and de whole woild
stops." Yank is in effect an absurdist figure, suddenly dimly aware of the
unbridgeable gulf between his simply conceived aspirations of harmony
and order and the refusal of the world to manifest it. He is stranded in a
world to which he cannot relate. He finds himself in a present which lacks
any casual relation to the past. As he senses, "I ain't got no past to tink in,
nor nothin' dat's comin', on'y what's now—and dat don't belong." For
O'Neill, as later for Beckett, the only moment of consonance is the
moment of death. As he slips to the floor, the author's stage direction
indicates that now, "perhaps, the Hairy Ape at least belongs."

The current always sweeps O'Neill's characters backwards, back to a
pre-social, pre-literate, pre-conscious past, in which primal emotions dominate, the complex arabesques of self defer to simple type, and language is
dismantled into phatic gestures. Brute existence exerts a gravitational pull
and his characters have little or no purchase on an alternative world.

For O'Neill, the space available for character to form, for language to
coalesce, and for social visions to expand, is minimal. The dominant image
is one of constriction. In *The Emperor Jones* the forest closes around the
protagonist, driving him back to meet the terrors of his own mind. In *The
Hairy Ape* character is reduced to type and compacted into a political,
moral and physical space which allows no scope for manoeuvre. "The
ceiling crushes down upon the men's heads. They can't stand upright."

MICHAEL MANHEIM

Remnants of a Cycle:
A Touch of the Poet
and More Stately Mansions

A TOUCH OF THE POET

Deceptively simple on the surface, *A Touch of the Poet* is actually among O'Neill's more complex plays and must be approached from a variety of directions. I shall therefore divide this discussion into three conventional categories—characters, plot, and dialogue—though these categories will be treated always in terms dictated by the theme of this study as a whole. My discussion of characters will focus on the "characters" of O'Neill's family, my discussion of plots will suggest that O'Neill was here departing from the past in the way he constructed a play, and my discussion of dialogue will deal with the reemerging rhythm of kinship.

Character

There should be little doubt that *A Touch of the Poet* is primarily a play about James O'Neill, Sr.: actor, father, and proud Irishman. Con Melody is a proud man who, having known success in earlier days, is now forced to live in what he considers undeserved obscurity. He is also like the old actor in that the past he recalls seems linked to the role O'Neill's father played throughout so much of his career. Con thinks of himself as having once been a kind of young Edmond Dantes in his brilliant Napoleonic uniform, and like that character Con feels wronged by ill-meaning adversaries, against whom he must seek revenge. Con, like James Tyrone, uses

From *Eugene O'Neill's New Language of Kinship*. © 1982 by Michael Manheim. Syracuse University Press, 1982.

his illusions about his glorious past to obscure his humble, shanty-Irish origins. Both behave like lords of a manor that exists more in their imaginations than in fact; and for both, the money needed to perpetuate their illusions is in short supply. It is their insistence upon living out their fantasies without the wherewithal to do so that irritates their outspoken offspring. Sara Melody, like the Tyrone brothers in regard to their father, views her voluble father as a figure who ought to "know better."

But Con's illusions go farther than do James's and take us into the realm of O'Neill's own problems rather than strictly his father's. Con's recall of the "Melody Castle" of his childhood—the very name suggesting its illusory nature—stands squarely for O'Neill's illusory recall of existence before the Fall, his earthly paradise with mother yet unstained. Similarly does the end of illusion as represented in this play have more to do with O'Neill himself than with his father. Con in the end must murder the little *mare* who symbolizes his aristocratic pipe dreams, as O'Neill knows that to bring himself back to reality he must rid himself permanently of memories of his mother (la mère). Con's shooting the mare late in the play, however, does not destroy memories, as O'Neill cannot destroy his memories. Rather, that shooting only reenacts once again O'Neill's fantasy killing of his mother, as Con's description of the dying mare makes clear:

> the look in her eyes by the lantern light with life ebbing out of them—wondering and sad, but still trusting, not reproaching me—with no fear in them—proud, understanding pride—loving me—she saw I was dying with her. She understood! She forgave me!

This is the image of the dying mother we [encounter] first in *The Great God Brown* and [hear] described in its ultimate form in *A Moon for the Misbegotten*. Thus, while Con obviously stands for O'Neill's father in his broader outlines, as Con's struggle with his illusions becomes critical, he stands more and more for O'Neill himself. We are back with O'Neill's old circle of hostility and guilt, even though in this play there is the clear desire to cast off, to exorcise, the memories that initiate its eternal recurrence.

Then there is Sara Melody, in whom O'Neill synthesizes the reactions to their father of both O'Neill brothers. Sara is an attractive, intelligent, articulate youth unwilling to accept the illusions of an older generation, especially as those illusions cause others to suffer. Yet also like the brothers, Sara is quite the prisoner of those same illusions, as she comes to realize by the end of the play. For all she tries to fight her similarity to

Con, it keeps breaking out, especially when Con shows signs of admitting what he is. Sara's identification with her father becomes particularly strong as Con finally does precisely what she has been urging him to do—face himself. She panics near the end because she realizes that her father's admitting he is nothing more than a brawling, conniving Irish shebeen-keeper makes her the conniving Irish wench she fears she really is. But she panics still more because she realizes that her father's new vulgarity in speech and behavior are as much a pose as was that of "Major Cornelius Melody." What she really fears, in short, is that both she and her father have *no* basic identity—that they are only what they decide to be for the moment, or conversely, that anything they decide to be is in the last analysis illusory. This same fear is repeated in Sara's thoughts about her lover Simon Harford. She can never resolve the dilemma over whether she truly loves Simon or is only after him for his money because that dilemma is unresolvable. Either alternative is true, or both alternatives are illusions which grow out of feelings of the moment. Sara is like the playwright wondering what is left when everything is revealed as illusion, the playwright who will shortly probe that problem so deeply in *The Iceman Cometh*. Sara is very much the rational part of O'Neill, and as such, like characters representing the rational O'Neill before her (Lavinia Mannon) and after (Larry Slade), carries her logic to inescapably despairing conclusions.

Nevertheless, Sara does not despair. Nora sees to that. "Shame on you to cry when you have love," says Nora to end the play and fulfill her inevitably sentimental function as all-Irish-American Earth Mother. Nora seems most akin to characters who are referred to but who never appear in other plays. It may be Marie Brantome described in *Mourning Becomes Electra* that O'Neill is trying to "bring to life" in Nora. It may also be the mother James Tyrone, Sr. describes in *Long Day's Journey*, the long-suffering Irish washer-woman who was O'Neill's paternal grandmother. This latter idea ties Nora more closely to Con as representative of the more earthy and open paternal side of O'Neill's background, and also allows her to be a version of the ideal mother O'Neill longed for and which he felt his more stable father actually had.

The problem with Nora is that she is just that—an ideal—and ideals tend to fare badly as dramatic characterizations. Nora's unvarying support and her predictable solutions to problems do little to enhance the otherwise convincing power of this play. It may well be that O'Neill, in recognition of this fact, created such later figures as Evelyn Hickman and the elder Mrs. Tyrone only in the descriptions of their husbands or sons.

Love represented in the near-saintly qualities of these women is more convincing when treated through memory. A truer representation of love in this play resides in dialogue involving Con himself—dialogue which is as hostile and explosive as it is spontaneous and loving.

Consistent with his practice of including qualities of his own mother even in his Earth Mothers, O'Neill also endows Nora with an overworked sense of guilt and a haunting fear. Here the cause of the guilt is not drugs, of course, but that other O'Neill bugaboo, illicit sex. Nora's guilt is over her premarital relations with Con. It is their special fear of church and priest that especially links Nora and Mary Tyrone. Neither is capable of confession, so terrible do they feel their sins have been. But even in guilt, Nora, unlike Mary, comes through as maudlin and conventional. The absence of a single aggressive reaction in Nora toward any member of her family suggests the limitations of her characterization.

Somewhat as he had with Aunt Lily in *Ah, Wilderness!*, O'Neill here creates a second female role more vividly to suggest his mother and her addictive state, a figure who assumes major prominence in this play's sequel. She is Deborah Harford, whose Yankee name and genteel breeding place her directly in the Quinlan-Mannon-Cavan tradition, as the name Melody may be associated with the names O'Neill, Brantome, and Tyrone. Deborah, who comes to forestall or delay her son's marriage into this shanty-Irish family, makes only a single appearance in the play, but it is a memorable one. Like Mary, she is delicate in appearance and exquisite in manner. She is attracted by the swashbuckling Con as the actor James Tyrone had once attracted the delicate Mary. Similarly, Deborah's rejection of Con's advances begins with her recognition of the liquor on his breath, as Mary's rejection of James first grew out of his drinking.

More to the point, however, is Deborah's tendency to withdraw. Here she is most like Mary. Even as she converses with Sara, she withdraws into her private world of dreams, that world she has inherited from her late father, an idealistic old revolutionary who finally found his long-sought "freedom" by withdrawing from all human intercourse into his "little Temple of Liberty," a small, enclosed retreat constructed in the corner of his garden. Deborah's struggles to avoid the same permanent withdrawal into that little Temple in this play and its sequel parallel Mary's struggles to stay out of her spare room, which similarly provides a freedom from life's severities. In addition, Deborah's illusions center on her being the secret mistress of Napoleon—a fantasy paralleling Mary's narcotic memories of her "affair" with the "Count of Monte Cristo."

O'Neill makes some changes in the Mannon-Brantome pattern here which he uses again in *Long Day's Journey* to suggest a basic similarity between his parents despite their more spectacular surface differences. Deborah's fantasies and withdrawal are presented as eccentricities which actually parallel Con's dreams of glory. Both recite Byron (Deborah in *More Stately Mansions*), both fancy themselves as isolated by their uniqueness, both come by very different routes from similarly humble origins. Immigrant peasant and Yankee lady are seen as living in essentially the same illusory condition—as O'Neill felt his shanty and lace-curtain progenitors both depended on quite similar illusions to maintain their equilibrium. This idea is picked up in *Long Day's Journey* in statements paralleling James's whiskey with Mary's morphine. It should be added, however, that as James never loses his grasp on reality, so Con always is aware of what he is doing. Deborah and Mary, on the other hand, do lose contact with reality, and hence the continuing difference in O'Neill's feelings about his father's difficulties and his mother's.

But the most surprising quality of Deborah Harford in this play is the essential lightness with which O'Neill treats her. That she verges on being a comic figure in her illusions suggests that O'Neill, as in *Ah, Wilderness!*, was trying to put his mother into perspective, a perspective lost anew in *More Stately Mansions*, where Deborah becomes a rather terrifying figure. In *A Touch of the Poet*, the bitterness so evident in O'Neill's treatment of the Mannons has become a kind of whimsical, detached amusement. O'Neill has here maintained a distance from his pain which allows him to make all the figures associated with it amusing. Of course, by the same token, the play's emotional penetration of its audience is also less than that of earlier and later plays, though it ranks high even in that regard among American family plays of the twentieth century.

So we have them again—the four figures of *Long Day's Journey*, with Jamie distinctly de-emphasized. The Jamie Cregan who is Con's former military subordinate is like Jamie Tyrone only in that he and the old campaigner seem continually in each other's company. O'Neill has carefully avoided putting any of the real Jamie's personality into him, perhaps for fear of upstaging Con, perhaps because the real Jamie was not so much on O'Neill's mind at the time he wrote this play.

Plots

More important, perhaps, than what O'Neill was doing with the major characters in this comedy is what he seems to be doing with its dramatic action. On the surface, its plot, or plots, [seem] to be borrowings, though this time not from anything resembling Aeschylus or Euripides. Instead of high tragedy, O'Neill is working here with various types of low comedy. One of its plots involves an Irish peasant father advising his daughter on how to trap a wealthy suitor into marriage by tricking him into having sexual relations with her. Another is about an Irish peasant humiliating an arrogant aristocrat. O'Neill would naturally be at ease with these plots in that they both come out of that same Irish folk-loristic tradition which had already inspired John Millington Synge and Sean O'Casey. As in the past, O'Neill uses ready-made plots as the framework for a great variety of emotional display; but here such plots are little more than humorous folk anecdotes, and the effect shifts from tears and anxiety in the earlier plays to action rich with Irish laughter in this one.

O'Neill's use of low comedy in the plotting of this play may grow in part out of O'Neill's growing sophistication about his art—and about himself. Con's hints that Sara take Simon Harford to bed and the spelled-out intricacy of Sara's efforts to that end have an obviousness about them which seems to suggest that we not take such manipulations seriously. And certainly Con's overwrought description of the revenge he intends to take on Simon's father is intended to evoke a far lighter response from the audience than it does from Con's anxious wife. There is a degree of mock melodrama in the play which evokes responses in us of a mixed variety. We may occasionally be concerned, but we are more often amused. In O'Neill's earlier plays, we were asked to take the characters as seriously as they took themselves. In this play, we are asked not to take them as seriously as they take themselves. Our perspective here is like that of Larry Slade on his tavern-mates in *The Iceman Cometh*—a kind of detached, even paternalistic, certainly amused devotion. Major Cornelius Melody thinks of himself as acting out a heroic revenge plot—something along the lines of *The Count of Monte Cristo*—but his audience knows that what is being re-enacted is actually an old Irish anecdote.

The increase in sophistication O'Neill asks of his audience in *A Touch of the Poet* may represent a further development of O'Neill's emotional and artistic growth. We have already seen something of that growth in the relative lightness with which he treats the chief character standing for his mother in the play, and certainly Con's activities reflect an objectivity regarding his father never before so evident. Con's revenge plot may also be a spoofing of O'Neill's own earlier melodramatic excesses. It may reflect O'Neill's feeling that his earlier plays were basically rather similar to his father's over-stated and over-produced vehicle. O'Neill's middle-period plots embody, after all, many of the same elements as *The Count of Monte Cristo.* The masking and unmasking of *The Great God Brown,* the deceptions and asides of *Strange Interlude,* the conspiracies and pursuits of *Mourning Becomes Electra* may all have been conscious or unconscious corollaries to the story of Edmond Dantes. In writing *A Touch of the Poet* O'Neill may be seeing in himself the pretentious emulator of his father. He may here be recognizing that in part at least he had been seeking to create the kind of stir his father had by using many of his father's methods. Such methods had worked for O'Neill, of course, very much as they had worked for his father. The comic vision comes with acceptance.

The notion of plots and plottings has another ramification as well. Sara plots and schemes a great deal in this play. She plots and schemes to get Simon Harford to marry her against his parents' wishes, and in this context she is oblivious to whether she loves him or not. To gain wealth and position, she says, she will "do anything"; and as a result the tone of her assault on the Harford name and fortune is wrapped in secretiveness and manipulation. Love, she says, has no place in such a package. But Sara does love Simon, and in describing her attempt to seduce Simon, she repeatedly speaks of how in his presence she forgets her schemes and gives way unabashedly to her feelings. What O'Neill implies here, in contrast to his middle period plays, is that when an authentic human relationship occurs, not the fulfillment merely of some previously conceived manipulation, the result is an uncontrollable flow of human emotion. Sara finds that in relation to Simon—and to her father in the final analysis—her immediate feelings must define her and that her plots and schemes only disguise her. Plotting is her means of deception, of herself as well as others, whereas spontaneous, open feeling is her best means of facing herself as well as others. The contrast between Sara's scheming and her outbursts of uncontrived love suggest an O'Neill increasingly aware that excessive plotting—by playwright perhaps as well as character—damages human beings, and that open confession of feeling—by playwright as well as character—saves.

Both the plots of *A Touch of the Poet* and the plottings in it are means by which characters perpetrate illusion. The abandonment of plotting and deceit is the means by which they survive. In this play, we get the first of several instances in O'Neill where the play comments on itself—and on the playwright's earlier work. O'Neill was to use similar material for the same purpose in writing *A Moon for the Misbegotten.*

Dialogue

The final question, then, is the nature of that which saves: the spontaneous, uncontrived responses of its central character toward those closest to him. The dialogue involving Con Melody almost parallels that in the all-but-plotless sea plays. We never see Sara with Simon, so her freely expressed love is merely an idyll as far as the play is concerned. That love is given no stage life because it is not represented in dialogue. The love which has living form on stage is not Sara's, nor even Nora's in her self-demeaning, maudlin expressions of support and affection, but Con's, in his explosive reactions to Nora—and to Sara. Con expresses his love by means of his constant, uncontrollable alternation of verbal abuse and verbal embrace. Typically, whenever Con's artistocratic illusions are questioned by his wife or daughter, he attacks viciously. But each attack is followed by a wave of regret, of apology, and of demonstrated affection. The more the hurt inflicted on him, the greater the attack, and the more sincere the reflex love. The resulting ebb and flow of emotion in Con's speeches seems more studied than what I have [called, elsewhere] the rhythm of kinship in the earlier plays, more part of O'Neill's conscious art. It seems here to be developing into a theatrical *language* of kinship, that language which will become the dominant language of his last plays. The following excerpt establishes a prevailing mood in this play against which all the plottings and deceptions so evident in earlier plays begin to seem paltry:

> MELODY: . . . I tried my best to educate you, after we came to America—until I saw it was hopeless.
> NORA: You did, surely. And I tried, too, but—
> MELODY: You won't even cure yourself of that damned peasant's brogue. And your daughter is becoming as bad.
> NORA: She only puts on the brogue to tease you. She can speak as fine as any lady in the land if she wants.
> MELODY: (*Is not listening—sunk in bitter brooding*) But, in God's name, who am I to reproach anyone with anything? Why don't you tell me to examine my own conduct?
> NORA: You know I'd never.
> MELODY: (*Stares at her—again he is moved—quietly*) No. I know you would not, Nora. (*He looks away—after a pause*) I owe you an apology for what happened last night.
> NORA: Don't think of it.

MELODY: (. . .) Faith, I'd a drink too many, talking over old times with Jamie Cregan.

NORA: I know.

MELODY: I am afraid I may have—the thought of old times—I become bitter. But you understand, it was the liquor talking, if I said anything to wound you.

NORA: I know it.

MELODY: (*Deeply moved* . . .) You're a sweet, kind woman, Nora—too kind. (*He kisses her*)

NORA: (. . .) Ah, Con darlin', what do I care what you say when the black thoughts are on you? Sure, don't you know I love you?

MELODY: (*A sudden revulsion of feeling convulses his face. He bursts out with disgust, pushing her away from him*) For God's sake, why don't you wash your hair? It turns my stomach with its stink of onions and stew! (. . .)

NORA: (*Dully*) I do be washin' it often to plaze you. But when you're standin' over the stove all day, you can't help—

MELODY: Forgive me, Nora. Forget I said that.

This passage is a good one because its flow of feeling is entirely natural while at the same time that flow seems carefully accounted for. The whole range of Con's emotions is present: the anger followed by the guilt followed by the dependency followed by the pride followed by the love—and all in turn followed by new irritation and new anger. There is no insult not followed by guilt, no forgiveness not followed by new insult. Everything said is meant sincerely, while no single emotion is dominant. Nor is any single emotion consistent with any other emotion. And the insult is never the "liquor talking" as Con is wont to say (along with Sid Davis, Hickey, the Tyrone men, and Erie Smith); it is always the man himself. But no less the man himself is the all-out expression of sorrow and love. As Con, with all his blather, is basically not a hypocrite, there are few hypocrites among O'Neill's later characters. Everything said in the heat of emotion is meant, and most things are spoken in the heat of emotion. Out of feelings stated in such a manner emerges O'Neill's new language of kinship.

The dialogue is dominated only by Con, however. Nora's patience can always be anticipated, as can Sara's spite where Con is involved. Nora's feelings never shift in response to Con, Sara's only occasionally. Sara has strong feelings, of course, but they are more like those in *Strange Inter-*

lude, reflected in asides and mini-soliloquies rather than spoken directly to Con, from whom she wishes to disguise her large measure of fellow feeling. In later plays, when O'Neill lets both parties to an emotional exchange go through the sudden shifts Con goes through here, sparks really fly, and concomitantly the sense of kinship is more deeply established. There is some of that between Sara and Con, but it is repeatedly checked by Sara's unwillingness to state her true feelings directly. She is the holdover from the middle period as far as her relationship with Con is concerned. And Nora's responses are all sentimentality. They never vary. It is Con's show throughout, as O'Neill intended it to be.

The basis of such dialogue as I have quoted from this play is found as early as the sea plays, but what one hears in those early plays is only O'Neill's fine sense of the basic rhythms of human communication. In this play we also become aware of a growing understanding of the way closely related human beings seek to communicate—as opposed to the ways they try not to communicate, which had been the central concern of O'Neill's middle period. And by communication alone, we begin to hear the plays suggesting, can man avoid or defer the horror his logical systems must lead him to.

Nevertheless, in spite of the sense of kinship created in this play, the undeniably loving portrait of its central figure, and its unlimited good humor, *A Touch of the Poet* really does end on a despairing note—as O'Neill, despite his efforts to the contrary, seems to have realized in *More Stately Mansions.* It is the same despair which nags at Seth's Shenandoah chanty and the "blessed isles" images in *Mourning Becomes Electra* and which will blossom forth in *The Iceman Cometh.* When one casts out illusion, what replaces it is also illusion—that, or total emptiness. Con's shebeen-keeper posture at the end of the play is every bit as much a pose as that of Major Cornelius Melody, as Sara realizes. The end of the play finds Con a seeming victor and Nora talking about hope through love, but the rational part remains unconvinced. Sara's perspective is finally the same as Larry Slade's. The happy endings of O'Neill's recent plays were beginning to run out, and with the return of O'Neill's gloom in the mid 1930s there were to be no more happy endings, no further attempts to "solve" the human dilemma. But by the same token, only *The Iceman Cometh* ends with a death, and that for quite specific reasons I shall treat [elsewhere]. In the other plays, the major characters—beaten, tired, almost lifeless—go on living, not in enclosures like Lavinia's mansion, but in the worlds they had already been inhabiting. They go on living possessed of frail new understandings born of the knowledge that they have been in authentic communication with another human being.

MORE STATELY MANSIONS

Two nine-act plays from the great cycle of which they were both a part intervened between the completion of *A Touch of the Poet* in 1936 and the first draft of *More Stately Mansions* in 1938; and whatever happened to O'Neill during their composition resulted in a return to despair which sentimentally optimistic elements in the unpublished typescript of the play do not allay. *More Stately Mansions* is a play about Simon Harford's failure in marriage, failure in business, and failure in understanding his relationship with his mother—all failures which follow what look for a time like bright prospects in each one of those enterprises.

Philosophically, *More Stately Mansions* points the way directly to *The Iceman Cometh*. The quasi-hopeful implications of Con Melody's rejection of his illusions in *A Touch of the Poet* are squelched in the scene which opens *More Stately Mansions* in the recorded version of its 1964 production in New York. In this scene Jamie Cregan is given a speech which makes clear not only a shift in Con's attitudes before his death but also in O'Neill's. Having tried to believe that man might be better off without his pipe dreams, O'Neill finally gave up the struggle. Says Jamie of Con:

> He could have drunk a keg a day and lived for twenty years
> yet, if the pride and spirit wasn't killed inside him ever since the
> night that he tried to challenge that Yankee coward Harford to
> a duel and him and me got beat by the police and arrested.

By the time he wrote this scene, O'Neill saw Con's "rehabilitation" the way he was to see that of the alcoholics at Harry Hope's saloon, as an experiment in cruel futility. And further, as nothing was left for Con but the quick, grim death O'Neill now envisions for him, so for most of mankind the so-called facing of reality must now be for O'Neill a short road to some form of meaningless self-annihilation. The ability to bear a totally absurd universe is reserved for only the very few—a very few who assume heroic dimensions in O'Neill's last plays.

The fixed, rational view of life's worthlessness in this play, begun with the report of Con's final days, is reinforced and varied through the statements and experiences of each of its central characters, as though O'Neill wished to keep the intellectual certainty of futility before us at all times— lest he slip back into sentimental ways. The Deborah Harford of this play, when she is not off on one of her periodic flights of fantasy, speaks with sobering clarity:

If life had meaning, then we might properly expect its end to have as much significance as—the period at the closing of a simple sentence, say. But it has no meaning, and that death is no more than the muddy well into which I and a dead cat are cast aside indifferently!

These views of Deborah's come to be shared by her son Simon, who perhaps more than any other character in O'Neill's plays suggests the author at his most tormented and his most cynical. Facing his own greed and lust after many years of considering himself an idealist, Simon concludes that the only real "evil" in the world is "the stupid theory that man is naturally what we call virtuous and good instead of being what he is, a hog." Following a pattern previously established by Orin Mannon and John Darling, Simon states that he is planning two books. These two books may stand for the two great periods of O'Neill's playwriting as he may have seen them in 1938: the first hopeful and idealistic, the second, like Orin's, increasingly hard-bitten and dominated by the total certainty of man's bankruptcy of spirit. But Simon goes farther than Orin. He even rejects his second book, nihilistic in its conclusions though it is, because any book at all would imply some lost worth to life, and all worth to Simon now, as to O'Neill, must be illusory.

Reinforcing Deborah's and Simon's explicit statements are the carefully arranged actions of the main characters, which most notably demonstrate the close relationship between making love and making money. Simon discovers the whole of man's rapacity present in himself and his wife. Despite his seeming commitment to ideals, his "touch of the poet," the grasping and treacherous side of Simon's nature must be predominant in the business world. What surprises Simon is not only that his time is increasingly occupied by his business activities, but that he also quite enjoys giving free rein to his rapacious side. He finds further that Sara's nature parallels his own. She seems to turn away from her maternal instincts and her natural altruism, and becomes cruel and manipulative once her acquisitive nature has been aroused. And it is her acquisitive nature, Simon becomes convinced, which is her basic nature, since she seems so adept at handling its demands. Similarly, although Deborah seems honest in her desire to be a good, loving grandmother, she has long been absorbed in fantasies which identify her as more possessive than Sara and quite as willing (though no longer able) to use her sexual attractions to acquire power. What the central characters do in the play, as well as what they say, seems amply to bear out their disquisitions on human corruptibility.

O'Neill's condemnation of the human spirit in this play is also evident in the character of Joel Harford, Simon's tight-lipped brother—a Lavinia Mannon who possesses none of the vitality O'Neill gives that earlier accuser. Joel is tempted sexually, as was Vinnie, but in him lust seems warped and paltry. It is never a sign, as it was in Vinnie, of healthy human impulses fighting their way through. Joel is a self-righteous moralist who considers that since he alone has a clear vision of "the right," he alone may pass judgment on others; and he does so with what he considers surgical precision. O'Neill obviously despises Joel most of all. If Simon stands for an O'Neill committing crimes against others out of a deep disillusionment with life, Joel is the vindictive O'Neill who is far worse because he refuses, or is afraid, ever to expose himself to an authentic human relationship. Joel's is the voice of a dessicated puritanism. O'Neill always hates the judge (in himself as in others) more than he does the sinner.

As usual, autobiography is central to the work. Although O'Neill here totally dismisses the image of his brother Jamie—the puritanical Joel is surely not such an image—his feelings about his late father's career are in evidence early in the play. Simon's late father, the successful Yankee trader, has ended his days in near bankruptcy. He had over-estimated his potential and engaged in opportunistic land deals—activities which certainly anticipate those of James Tyrone, Sr. Simon absorbs his father's company, taking on himself the reputation of the Harford name, as by the time this play was written O'Neill has totally overshadowed his father's reputation in his father's own field. O'Neill's feelings about his father are thus rather precisely if minimally represented in *More Stately Mansions*.

Also as usual, the more important action of the play relates to O'Neill's complex of feelings associated with his mother. Following the familiar pattern, Deborah resembles Mary Tyrone physically, and like Mary she has fantasies into which she withdraws when life is too much for her. Deborah's dreams of being a "rich adventuress" in the court of Napoleon parallel Mary's dream of her courtship by the "Count of Monte Cristo," and the "little Temple of Liberty" to which Deborah withdraws certainly parallels Mary's spare room and all the horrors associated with it in O'Neill's mind. Deborah is still more like Mary in the increasing impenetrability of her withdrawals. Deborah senses the oncoming permanence of her condition in terms which precisely express what O'Neill imagines as his mother's state of mind in *Long Day's Journey*. Looking forward to her fate at the end of the play, Deborah says:

in the end—and I have reached the end—the longing for a
moment's unthinking peace, a second's unquestioning acceptance of one's self, becomes so terrible that I would do anything, give anything to escape! . . . The temptation to escape—
open the door—step boldly across the threshold.

. . . .

It would be easy for me! Like pushing open a door in the mind
and then passing through the freedom of one's lifelong desire!

The fear of a mother's permanent withdrawal is still the context of
O'Neill's greatest pain.

But there is a difference between O'Neill's treatment of his old agony
in this play and in earlier plays. Here, as in *A Touch of the Poet*, O'Neill
seems more detached and self-controlled in dealing with his pain. In *A
Touch of the Poet*, that more detached quality revealed itself in lightness
and humor. Here there is an underlying scientific, or would-be scientific,
tone. Emotions feel numbed in this play, and O'Neill seems bent on
examining them in their numbed state with a precision which, ironically
perhaps, suggests Joel's precision. O'Neill seems determined throughout
most of this play to understand first of all his conflicting fantasies—fantasies
associated with the past, and fantasies associated with the present. His
fantasies associated with the past, of course, derive from thoughts about
his mother—those associated with the present, with thoughts about his
problems as husband, father, and provider. The main body of the play
reveals first his attempt to reconcile these conflicting fantasies, and finally,
in his failure to reconcile them, his resulting panic and despair.

Acts two and three in a highly schematic manner dramatize O'Neill's
attempt to reconcile his fantasies, then his failure to reconcile them. These
two acts are divided into scenes of three types: the first revealing O'Neill's
fantasies relating to his marriage, the second his fantasies relating to his
mother, and the third his fantasies growing out of his sense of isolation.
The first type focuses naturally on Simon and Sara, the second on Simon
and Deborah, and the third on Simon responding to Sara and Deborah as
one. The third type deals with thoughts and feelings which represent the
author's suicidal despair.

The scenes involving Simon and Sara and those involving Simon and
Deborah at first seem simply enough conceived. Unable to sleep with his
wife because of the presence of his mother and unable to be happy with his
mother because of the presence of his wife, Simon invites his wife to live
out his sexual fantasies with him at his office and lives out his childhood

fantasies by paying brief visits to his mother in her garden. As part of his sexual fantasies, Sara must play the role of whore, in ritual fashion winning from him all his business holdings in return for her sexual favors, and as part of his childhood fantasies, Deborah must treat him like a little boy. Sara accepts his invitation, thus revealing the immorally acquisitive side of her nature; and Deborah accepts his visits, thus revealing that side of her nature which will not accept the present. That these are O'Neill's conflicting fantasies seems clear. As they had ten years earlier, memories of his mother were ruining O'Neill's sex life, or, conversely, the persistent amorous demands of a wife were interfering with his reveries about an idealized distant past with his mother.

But Simon's (O'Neill's) fantasies are only a part of what these scenes are about—and, in the final analysis, a small part. Simon is indeed tormented by his childhood fantasies to the extent that he cannot have an adult relationship with his wife and by his sexual fantasies to the extent that he cannot treat his mother with mature filial affection. But at the same time, he loves his wife and he loves his mother in ways that have nothing to do with his fantasies. A large part of him wants his wife to be happy—not as an acquisitive whore but as a companion and mother to his children. And a large part of him, the same large part in fact, wants his mother to be happy and fulfilled as an affectionate grandmother. And as with Simon, so with Sara and Deborah. They have natures which exist quite apart from their fantasies. A large part of Sara wants to be loving wife and mother, and a large part of Deborah wants to be affectionate grandmother and wise counselor. These more immediate, down-to-earth qualities in the characters exist side by side with their fantasies right through all these scenes.

At the heart of these scenes is the thought that whatever any character does or says is only one-half of what they are at any particular moment. Simon's sexuality (not his sexual fantasies) is one-half loving desire and one-half greed. And that similarly acquisitive "little boy" half when he is with his mother is one-half genuine desire for love of which he was earlier deprived and one-half a compulsive need for withdrawal, like his mother's. Similarly, Sara's whore/tycoon half is one-half sensible and one-half grasping, and her wife-motherly half is one-half supportive and one-half possessive. By the same token, Deborah's withdrawing half is one-half imaginatively creative and one-half selfish, and her grandmotherly half is one-half supportive and one-half possessive (here like Sara, naturally). Equally important is the fact that all these various halves do not exist in any kind of ironic relationship to their opposites. Each half exists side by side with its opposing half, without commenting on it in any way. Again and again, characters are startled to realize the bifurcations in their responses—but there is nothing to be learned from these bifurcations other than that they exist. Very little hypocrisy is involved in any of these characters. Simon thinks that Sara and Deborah are being hypocritical when they are being affectionate toward one another, but both lines and stage directions make clear that the affection they state is usually genuine. The halvings are always at work in the play. Each half of each response is separate and true, and each half is itself subject, as it were, to surgical bisection. As one examines these scenes more and more closely, one gets the sense of a seemingly endless series of possible halvings.

These halvings are part of the socio-historical message of O'Neill's great, lost cycle, in which he was intent upon developing the theme that all those impulses which brought about the achievements of our national past were at least one part possessive, and that this history of unrelenting acquisitiveness was what was now (in the 1930s) dispossessing Americans. But it is the *other* sets of halves which holds greater interest for me—those qualities which are the opposite of the rapacity and the whoring. Quite contradictory kinds of responses reveal the true state of O'Neill's consciousness in writing this play and the plays that follow it. Sara, early in the recorded production, speaks of admiring her late father for his "defiance of a God he denied but really believed in." It takes a while to appreciate the number of contradictions this idea implies. I only wish to note that the statement includes Con's abiding belief. It is that same abiding belief, I suspect, that underlies the many humane and loving responses and actions in the play—the familial responses of Sara and Deborah, for example, or Deborah's suddenly pushing Simon away from her little Temple at the end of the play. One half a violent gesture of paranoid withdrawal, the latter is also one half the all-out sacrifice of a mother protecting her child from a terrible fate. As I have said, there seems nothing anyone says or does of an evil nature in this play which is not countered by an opposing act or statement. The question comes to be, do these counterings not in the end simply cancel human existence out, reduce it to Samuel Beckett's absolute zero? In this play and its successor, O'Neill vehemently *says* yes, but never quite *means* yes—a division which itself accords with the play's basic duality. Like Con Melody, O'Neill is always defying a faith he denies but never yields.

The Simon who plots and manipulates separate and grotesque relationships with wife and mother is very much the O'Neill of the middle period perceived now with greater objectivity—as, say, William Brown was never perceived. O'Neill *is* Simon, but he is also looking *at* Simon with clinical detachment. This detachment is perhaps most evident in the play's most memorable scene. The scene is of the third type referred to earlier, that which deals with Simon's (O'Neill's) suicidal sense of isolation. To escape his isolation in earlier plays, O'Neill frequently had his central character search for an Earth Mother—a total provider, a bringer of comfort, a figure in all respects, physical and emotional, more powerful than himself. In act two, scene three, Deborah and Sara unite to become that figure, a development which reenacts O'Neill's old fantasy. But united, Deborah and Sara become not a blissful fantasy but an image inspiring only terror. The fantasy of mother and wife fused into a single person, which appears in one form or another in many O'Neill plays, becomes here a new center of panic rather than of comfort. Instead of feeling restored, Simon feels completely isolated by this fusion of personalities. He feels shut out by this new image of the Earth Mother even as she embraces him.

In the scene in question (act two, scene three), the idea of characters fusing and separating is enacted with characteristic precision as the motherly halves of Deborah and Sara coalesce to master as they isolate the desperate Simon. Each of the scene's three characters, in interior monologue, ruminates over his or her contrapuntal desires and suspicions. All three seem isolated and deeply troubled to begin with, though it is Simon alone who remains in this state throughout the scene. First, Deborah and Sara cease being separate individuals and become a single individual whose existence drives Simon to the edge of panic. They taunt him like harpies, then they confront him "with the calculating coquetry of two prostitutes." Then they break apart, temporarily releasing Simon from the torment they have put him in, though the release is brief, since they will shortly coalesce again to drive Simon over the edge of his abyss. But even now, the torment they inflict as separate individuals is little better than that which they inflicted as a single individual. Simon cannot stand the fusion of mother and wife, but he also cannot stand them as separate, violently conflicting identities—the problem that started his troubles to begin with. Hence the fantasy suicide which this scene intimates and which the final act of the play enacts.

But again, despair and panic pointing toward a fantasy suicide is only half of what this scene enacts. There is here, as everywhere else, the opposing half. Even as the scene dissects its author's overwhelming fear, it also describes the nature of his irrepressible faith. It is a scene that tells us as much about how people survive as about how they do not survive. As I stated earlier, the union of Sara and Deborah may in one sense simply reflect a highly disturbed state of mind, but the two figures are also represented in their "fusion" as quite distinct characters who suddenly find much-needed support from one another. The love they generate in one another feels authentic:

> SARA: (*Thinking—resentfully*) Poor woman! She can't read—she's thinking how she'll miss the children alone all day—He'll have me at the office—Alone in the past—He'll have her in an asylum in the end!—It's a terrible thing he can hate his mother so!—
>
> DEBORAH: (*Thinking*) She had begun to look upon me as a second mother—and I was happy to regard her as my daughter—because her strength and health and acceptance of life gave me a faith in my own living—and now he dares to take that security away from me!—to offer me in exchange ghosts from the past to haunt me—
>
> SARA: (*Thinking*) I'm not a thought he moves around in his mind to suit his pleasure—
>
> DEBORAH: (*Thinking*) If she'd sit with me here as on other nights, we'd understand and forgive each other—(*They both speak to each other simultaneously: "Sara" "Deborah" They bend forward so they can see each other past him and smile at each other with a relieved understanding. Deborah speaks with strange gentleness*)
> Yes, Daughter. I ought to have known you guessed my thoughts.
>
> SARA: (*Getting up—with a quiet smile*) I hope you guessed mine. May I come and sit with you?
>
> DEBORAH: I was going to ask you. (*Sara goes around the table and passes behind Simon, ignoring him, and goes to the sofa. Deborah pats the sofa on her left, smiling an affectionate welcome*)
> This is your place, beside me.

There is nothing these lines tell us other than that along with their feelings of hatred for one another, Sara and Deborah have feelings of mutual affection—genuine feelings of affection. Simon's is the distorted set of reactions, the "strange" element in the scene despite the use of that word in describing the women. Simon remains in isolation; they do not. His honesty with the audience is honesty only with himself in his spoken

inner thoughts. Sara and Deborah communicate honestly with one another, both in their affection here demonstrated and in their hostility.
Their coming together and their separating is something more than fantasy. It is also an enactment of the processes of kinship, and the self-
defined odd-man-out is the only real sufferer. The alternating hostility and
affection between Sara and Deborah makes them as well off as Simon is
badly off. The scene tells us finally as much about people in the polyphony
of kinship as it does about O'Neill's fantasies and despair.

Kinship is what O'Neill, knowingly or not, seems to be working
toward in this play even as he is attempting to certify the folly of any kind
of philosophical truth. Simon protests the total meaninglessness of things
while others move toward authentic human relationships. Simon insists
upon keeping his halves divided—which some would call schizophrenia—
while others let their similar halves unite and their opposing halves do
battle. In the relationship of Sara and Deborah the matrix of kinship is
more systematically presented than in any other previous play. In *More
Stately Mansions*, O'Neill seems on the verge of transcending his agony
even as he seems most immersed in it. Still, he does not transcend it.
O'Neill through Simon continues battering at the interior wall of his old
imprisoning circle. Simon's blow to the head near the end of the play, the
result of his mother's efforts to protect him from her fate, seems to
promise some basic change in his direction—but the blow to the head
quickly becomes the old reenactment of O'Neill's original disillusionment.
The blow comes from his mother, and thus is O'Neill still trapped by the
past. We are back with Orin Mannon, permanently bewildered by the old
wound to the head. The state in which O'Neill leaves his hero in *More
Stately Mansions* is in fact the worst of human conditions. Simon's fate is
like that of Oswald Alving in Ibsen's *Ghosts*. Having avoided suicide or
madness—his desire to join his mother in her little Temple could mean
either—Simon becomes a vegetable. O'Neill, in his efforts to reach a
bedrock level of existence without illusion, has now descended for his
central image to that of a semi-conscious invalid needing the literal
ministrations of a *nurse*-mother.

In its explicitness, *More Stately Mansions* may be the most informa-
tive among O'Neill's plays. Here alone does a figure standing squarely for
the author obviously use the study of himself as the basis for his understanding of others. Simon is like Shakespeare's King Richard II in prison
"hammering out" the structure of his despair, "peopling his world with
little thoughts," descanting on the meaninglessness of existence. Having
gone through the pretense of accepting false solutions, O'Neill is

philosophically back where he was at the conclusion of *Mourning Becomes Electra*. But whether he would or no, the despair could not erase his strong sense of the emotional pulsations of people in close relationships. Rather than being at the end of his road as an artist, he was actually at the point where he might be ready to combine the two contradictory forces that had dominated all his plays—his despair and his sense of the rhythm of kinship. His skill at writing plays, and his reasons for writing them, were very great. But one more element was needed, a reason to genuinely consider himself a playwright of the largest tragic magnitude. Something was needed to make O'Neill feel that the autobiographical agony and the vison of kinship were of true worth to mankind—and that something may have been his winning the Nobel Prize in 1936.

Chronology

1888	October 16, in New York City, Eugene Gladstone O'Neill is born to James O'Neill, a well-known actor, and Ella Quinlan.
1902	O'Neill enters Betts Academy in Stamford, Connecticut.
1906–7	Attends Princeton.
1909	Marries Kathleen Jenkins; goes prospecting for gold in Honduras.
1910	Son Eugene Gladstone O'Neill, Jr., is born. O'Neill sails for Buenos Aires.
1912	Divorces Kathleen Jenkins. Begins work as a reporter for *New London Telegraph*. Publishes poetry. Enters Gaylord Farm, tuberculosis sanatorium, for a six-month stay.
1913	*A Wife for Life* and *The Web*, O'Neill's first plays, are copyrighted.
1914	O'Neill's father helps to pay for the publication of *Thirst*, a volume of five one-act plays.
1916	Provincetown Players produce *Bound East for Cardiff*, *Thirst*, and *Before Breakfast*.
1917	*Fog*, *The Sniper*, *In the Zone*, *The Long Voyage Home*, and *Ile* are produced.
1918	O'Neill marries Agnes Boulton and moves to Cape Cod. *The Rope*, *Where the Cross Is Made*, and *The Moon of the Caribbees* are produced.

1919   *The Dreamy Kid* is produced. Son Shane is born.

1920   *Beyond the Horizon* is produced and wins the Pulitzer Prize. *Chris Christoferson* (first version of *Anna Christie*), *Exorcism*, *The Emperor Jones*, and *Diff'rent* produced.

1921   *Gold, The Straw*, and *Anna Christie* produced. *Anna Christie* wins Pulitzer Prize, O'Neill's second.

1922   *The First Man* and *The Hairy Ape* produced.

1924   *Welded, The Ancient Mariner, All God's Chillun Got Wings, S.S. Glencairn*, and *Desire under the Elms* are produced.

1925   *The Fountain* produced. Daughter Oona is born.

1926   *The Great God Brown* produced. O'Neill receives an honorary Litt.D. from Yale University.

1928   *Marco Millions, Strange Interlude*, and *Lazarus Laughed* are produced. Wins third Pulitzer for *Strange Interlude*. Divorces again.

1929   O'Neill marries Carlotta Monterey. *Dynamo* is produced. Moves to Le Plessis, France.

1931   *Mourning Becomes Electra* is produced.

1932   Returns to U.S. and builds Casa Genotta, in Sea Island, Georgia.

1933   *Ah, Wilderness!* is produced.

1934   *Days without End* produced.

1936   O'Neill wins the Nobel Prize for literature.

1937   Moves to California, where he builds Tao House.

1946   *The Iceman Cometh* is produced.

1947   O'Neill diagnosed as having Parkinson's Disease. *A Moon for the Misbegotten* is produced.

1950   Son Eugene O'Neill, Jr., dies.

1953   O'Neill develops pneumonia and dies on November 27 in Boston.

1956   *Long Day's Journey into Night* is produced. Jose Quintero revives *The Iceman Cometh*.

1957   *A Touch of the Poet* is produced.

1958   *Hughie* is produced.

1962   *More Stately Mansions* is produced.

Contributors

HAROLD BLOOM, Sterling Professor of the Humanities at Yale University, is the author of *The Anxiety of Influence, Poetry and Repression*, and many other volumes of literary criticism. His forthcoming study, *Freud: Transference and Authority*, attempts a full-scale reading of all of Freud's major writings. A MacArthur Prize Fellow, he is general editor of five series of literary criticism published by Chelsea House.

LIONEL TRILLING, University Professor at Columbia University, was one of the most eminent critics in American literary history. His works include *The Liberal Imagination, Beyond Culture*, and *Sincerity and Authenticity*.

DORIS FALK is Professor Emeritus of English at Rutgers University. In addition to her work on O'Neill, she has written a major volume on Lillian Hellman.

ARNOLD GOLDMAN has written several books on James Joyce and is the general editor of the *American Literature in Context* series.

ROBERT C. LEE teaches at the American University in Paris.

TRAVIS BOGARD is Professor of Dramatic Art at the University of California, Berkeley. His works include *The Tragic Satire of John Webster* and volume eight, on American drama, of Ravel's *History of Drama in English*.

THOMAS F. VAN LAAN is Professor of English at Rutgers University. He is the author of *Role Playing in Shakespeare*.

JEAN CHOTHIA is Fellow and Assistant Lecturer in English at Selwyn College, Cambridge. She is the author of *Forging a Language*.

C. W. E. BIGSBY is Reader in the School of English and American Studies at the University of East Anglia. He has edited *Superculture* and *Approach* to *Popular Culture* and is the author of *Confrontation and Commitment, Dada and Surrealism,* and *Tom Stoppard.*

MICHAEL MANHEIM is Professor of English at the University of Toledo, in Ohio, and author of *The Weak King Dilemma in the Shakespearean History Play* and *Eugene O'Neill's Language of Kinship.*

Bibliography

Adler, Thomas P. "Through a Glass Darkly: O'Neill's Esthetic Theory as Seen through His Writer Characters." *Arizona Quarterly* 32 (1976): 171–83.

Alexander, Doris. "Strange Interlude and Schopenhauer." *American Literature* 25 (1953): 213–28.

———. *The Tempering of Eugene O'Neill.* New York: Harcourt, Brace & World, 1962.

Barlow, Judith E. *Final Acts: The Creation of Three Late O'Neill Plays.* Athens: The University of Georgia Press, 1985.

Bentley, Eric. "Trying to Like O'Neill." *The Kenyon Review* 14, no. 3 (1952): 476–92.

Berlin, Normand. *Eugene O'Neill.* New York: Grove Press, 1982.

Bogard, Travis. *Contour in Time: The Plays of Eugene O'Neill.* New York: Oxford University Press, 1972.

Bowen, Croswell. *The Curse of the Misbegotten: A Tale of the House of O'Neill.* New York: McGraw-Hill, 1959.

Broussard, Louis. *American Drama: Contemporary Allegory from Eugene O'Neill to Tennessee Williams.* Norman: University of Oklahoma Press, 1962.

Brustein, Robert. *The Theatre of Revolt: An Approach to the Modern Drama.* Boston: Little, Brown, 1964.

Cargill, Oscar, N. Bryllion Fagin, and William J. Fisher, eds. *O'Neill and His Plays: Four Decades of Criticism.* New York: New York University Press, 1961.

Carpenter, Frederic. *Eugene O'Neill.* Rev. ed. Boston: Twayne, 1979.

Chabrowe, Leonard. *Ritual and Pathos: The Theater of O'Neill.* Lewisburg, Pa.: Bucknell University Press, 1976.

Chothia, Jean. *Forging a Language: A Study of the Plays of Eugene O'Neill.* London: Cambridge University Press, 1979.

Clark, Barrett H. *Eugene O'Neill: The Man and His Plays.* Rev. ed.: New York: Dover, 1947.

Clark, Marden J. "The Tragic Effect in *The Hairy Ape*." *Modern Drama* 10 (1968): 372–82.

Cooley, John R. "*The Emporer Jones* and the Harlem Renaissance." *Studies in Literary Imagination* 7 (1974): 73–83.

Coolidge, Olivia. *Eugene O'Neill.* New York: Scribner's, 1966.

Engel, Edwin A. *The Haunted Heroes of Eugene O'Neill.* Cambridge: Harvard University Press, 1953.

Falk, Doris V. *Eugene O'Neill and the Tragic Tension: An Interpretive Study of the Plays.* New Brunswick, N.J.: Rutgers University Press, 1958.

Floyd, Virginia, ed. *Eugene O'Neill: A World View.* New York: Frederick Ungar, 1979.

————. *The Plays of Eugene O'Neill: A New Assessment.* New York: Frederick Ungar, 1985.

Frenz, Horst. *Eugene O'Neill.* Berlin: Collquium Verlag, 1965.

Gassner, John. *Eugene O'Neill.* Minneapolis: University of Minnesota Press, 1965.

————. *Form and Idea in the Modern Theatre.* New York: Holt, Rinehart & Winston, 1956.

————. *O'Neill: A Collection of Critical Essays.* Englewood Cliffs, N.J.: Prentice-Hall, 1964.

Gelb, Arthur, and Barbara Gelb. *O'Neill.* Enl. ed. New York: Harper & Row, 1973.

Glicksberg, Charles I. *The Tragic Vision in Twentieth Century Literature.* Carbondale: Southern Illinois University Press, 1963.

Griffin, Ernest. *Eugene O'Neill: A Collection of Criticism.* New York: McGraw-Hill, 1976.

Grimm, Reinhold. "A Note on O'Neill, Nietzsche and Naturalism: *Long Day's Journey Into Night* in European Perspective." *Modern Drama* 26 (1983): 331–34.

Heilman, Robert. *The Iceman, the Arsonist and the Troubled Agent.* Seattle: University of Washington Press, 1973.

Kafchick, Marcellino. "Film and Fiction in O'Neill's *Hughie.*" *Arizona Quarterly* 39 (1983): 47–61.

Krutch, Joseph Wood. *The American Drama Since 1918.* Rev. ed. New York: Braziller, 1957.

Leech, Clifford. *Eugene O'Neill.* New York: Grove Press, 1963.

Long, Chester Clayton. *The Role of Nemesis in the Structure of Selected Plays by Eugene O'Neill.* The Hague: Mouton, 1968.

Manheim, Michael. "O'Neill's Transcendence of Melodramas in *A Touch of the Poet* and *A Moon for the Misbegotten.*" *Comparative Drama* 10 (1982): 238–50.

Metzger, Deena P. "Variations on a Theme: A Study of *Exiles* by James Joyce and *The Great God Brown* by Eugene O'Neill." *Modern Drama* 8 (1965): 174–84.

Miller, Jordan Y. *Eugene O'Neill and the American Critic: A Summary and Bibliographical Checklist.* Hamden, Conn.: Shoe String, 1962.

————. *Playwright's Progress: O'Neill and the Critics.* Chicago: Scott, Foresman & Company, 1965.

Moleski, Joseph. "Eugene O'Neill and the Cruelty of Theater." *Comparative Drama* 15, no. 4 (1981–82): 327–42.

Nathan, George Jean. "Portrait of O'Neill." In *O'Neill and His Plays*, edited by Oscar Cargill, 50–64. New York: New York University Press, 1961.

Raleigh, John Henry. *The Plays of Eugene O'Neill.* Carbondale: Southern Illinois University Press, 1965.

————, ed. *Twentieth Century Interpretations of "The Iceman Cometh": A Collection of Critical Essays.* Englewood, N.J.: Prentice-Hall, 1968.

Robinson, James A. *Eugene O'Neill and Oriental Thought: A Divided Vision.* Carbondale: Southern Illinois University Press, 1982.

Scheibler, Rolf. *The Late Plays of Eugene O'Neill.* Bern: A. Francke, 1970.

Sewall, Richard B. *The Vision of Tragedy.* Rev. and enl. ed. New Haven: Yale University Press, 1980.

Shawcross, John T. "The Road To Ruin: The Beginning of O'Neill's *Long Day's Journey.*" *Modern Drama* 3 (1960): 289–96.

Sheaffer, Louis. *O'Neill: Son and Artist.* Boston: Little, Brown, 1973.

Shipley, Joseph T. *The Art of Eugene O'Neill.* Seattle: University of Washington Chapbooks, 1928.

Shurr, William H. "American Drama and the Bible: The Case of Eugene O'Neill's *Lazarus Laughed.*" In *The Bible and American Arts and Letters,* edited by Giles Gunn, 83–103. Philadelphia: Fortress, 1983.

Sievers, W. David. *Freud on Broadway; A History of Psychoanalysis and the American Drama.* New York: Hermitage House, 1955.

Skinner, Richard Dana. *Eugene O'Neill: A Poet's Quest.* New York: Russell & Russell, 1964.

Sproxton, Birk. "Eugene O'Neill: Masks and Demons." *Sphinx* 3 (1975): 57–62.

Stamm, Rudolf. " 'Faithful Realism': Eugene O'Neill and the Problem of Style." *English Studies* 40 (1959): 242–50.

Strickland, Edward. "Baudelaire's 'Portraits de Maitresses' and O'Neill's *The Iceman Cometh.*" *Romance Notes* 22 (1982): 291–94.

Tiusanen, Timo. *O'Neill's Scenic Images.* Princeton: Princeton University Press, 1968.

Törnqvist, Egil. "Ibsen and O'Neill: A Study in Influence." *Scandinavian Studies* 37 (1965): 211–35.

———. *A Drama of Souls: Studies in O'Neill's Super-Naturalistic Technique.* New Haven: Yale University Press, 1969.

Waith, Eugene M. "Eugene O'Neill: An Exercise in Unmasking." *Educational Theater Journal* 13, no. 3 (1961): 182–91.

Watson, James. "The Theater in *The Iceman Cometh*: Some Modernist Implications." *Arizona Quarterly* 34 (1978): 230–38.

Wichler, Stephen. "O'Neill's Long Journey." *Commonweal* 63 (1956): 614–15.

Wiles, Timothy J. "Tammanyite, Progressive and Anarchist: Political Communities in *The Iceman Cometh.*" *CLIO: A Journal of Literature, History and the Philosophy of History* 9 (1979): 179–96.

Winther, Sophus Keith. "*Desire under the Elms*: A Modern Tragedy." *Modern Drama* 3 (1960): 326–32.

———. *Eugene O'Neill: A Critical Study.* 2d ed. New York: Random House, 1961.

Acknowledgments

"Eugene O'Neill" by Lionel Trilling from *Essays in Modern Drama* edited by Morris Freedman, © 1936 by the *New Republic*.

"Fatal Balance: O'Neill's Last Plays" (originally entitled "Fatal Balance") by Doris Falk from *Eugene O'Neill and the Tragic Tension* by Doris Falk, © 1958 by Rutgers, the State University. Reprinted by permission of Rutgers University Press.

"The Vanity of Personality: The Development of Eugene O'Neill" by Arnold Goldman from *American Theatre* (Stratford Upon Avon Series), © 1967 by Edward Arnold (Publishers) Ltd. Reprinted by permission.

"Evangelism and Anarchy in *The Iceman Cometh*" by Robert C. Lee from *Modern Drama* 12, no. 2 (September 1969), © 1969 by the University of Toronto, Graduate School for the Study of Drama. Reprinted by permission.

"The Historian: *Mourning Becomes Electra* and *Ah! Wilderness*" by Travis Bogard from *Contour in Time* by Travis Bogard, © 1972 by Oxford University Press. Reprinted by permission.

"Singing in the Wilderness: The Dark Vision of O'Neill's Only Mature Comedy" (originally entitled Singing in the Wilderness: The Dark Vision of Eugene O'Neill's Only Mature Comedy") by Thomas F. Van Laan from *Modern Drama* 22, no. 1 (March 1979), © 1978 by the University of Toronto, Graduate Centre for the Study of Drama. Reprinted by permission.

"*Long Day's Journey into Night*: The Dramatic Effectiveness of Supposedly Neutral Dialogue" (originally entitled "Significant Form: *Long Day's Journey into Night*") by Jean Chothia from *Forging a Language: A Study of the Plays of Eugene O'Neill* by Jean Chothia, © 1979 by Cambridge University Press. Reprinted by permission.

"Four Early Plays" (originally entitled "Race and the Dramatization of the Unconscious") by C. W. E. Bigsby from *Twentieth-Century American Drama 1900–1940*, vol. 1, by C. W. E. Bigsby, © 1982 by Cambridge University Press. Reprinted by permission.

"Remnants of a Cycle: *A Touch of the Poet* and *More Stately Mansions*" by Michael Manheim from *Eugene O'Neill's New Language of Kinship* by Michael Manheim, © 1982 by Michael Manheim. Reprinted by permission of Syracuse University Press, Syracuse, New York.

Index